Distributed
Leadership

James P. Spillane

Distributed Leadership

JOSSEY-BASS
A Wiley Imprint
www.josseybass.com

Published by Jossey-Bass
A Wiley Imprint
989 Market Street, San Francisco, CA 94103-1741   www.josseybass.com

Jossey-Bass books and products are available through most bookstores. To contact Jossey-Bass directly call our Customer Care Department within the U.S. at 800-956-7739, outside the U.S. at 317-572-3986, or fax 317-572-4002.

Jossey-Bass also publishes its books in a variety of electronic formats. Some content that appears in print may not be available in electronic books.

Library of Congress Cataloging-in-Publication Data
Spillane, James P.
  Distributed leadership / James P. Spillane.—1st ed.
     p. cm. — (The Jossey-Bass leadership library in education)
  Includes bibliographical references and index.
  ISBN-13: 978-0-7879-6538-9 (alk. paper)
  ISBN-10: 0-7879-6538-3 (alk. paper)
  1. Educational leadership—United States. 2. School management and organization—United States. I. Title. II. Series.
  LB2805.S745 2006
  371.2—dc22   2005017309

THE JOSSEY-BASS
Leadership Library in Education

•

Andy Hargreaves
Consulting Editor

THE JOSSEY-BASS LEADERSHIP LIBRARY IN EDUCATION is a distinctive series of original, accessible, and concise books designed to address some of the most important challenges facing educational leaders. The authors are respected thinkers in the field who bring practical wisdom and fresh insight to emerging and enduring issues in educational leadership. Packed with significant research, rich examples, and cutting-edge ideas, these books will help both novice and veteran leaders understand their practice more deeply and make schools better places to learn and work.

ANDY HARGREAVES is the Thomas More Brennan Chair in Education in the Lynch School of Education at Boston College and the author of numerous books on culture, change, and leadership in education.

For current and forthcoming titles in the series, please see the last pages of this book.

Contents

Acknowledgments

Authorship often fails to reflect that books are collaborative endeavors; the pages that follow have benefited from the work of
many hands and minds. Special thanks go to the teachers and
school leaders who opened up their schools, allowing my research
team to attend meetings, sit in classrooms, and generally hang out
over a period of five years. As a tribute to their generosity, this first
book from the Distributed Leadership Study is about the practice
of leadership.

This book would not have been possible without the contributions of an outstanding interdisciplinary research team of postdoc-
toral fellows, graduate students, and undergraduate students at
Northwestern University. I am especially grateful to John Diamond,
who served as my project director for the Distributed Leadership
Study. Special thanks also go to Patricia Burch, Lawrence Bren-
ninkmeyer, Fred Brown, Loyiso Jita, Richard Halverson, Jennifer
Sherer, Amy Coldren, Tim Hallett, Tondra Loder, and Antonia
Randolph.

This book also would not have been possible without the gen-
erous financial support for the Distributed Leadership Study from
the National Science Foundation (REC-9873583) and the
Spencer Foundation (200000039). Special thanks go to Jim Dietz
and Elizabeth Vanderputten at the National Science Foundation
for their ongoing support for the project and for their challenging

questions. Northwestern University's School of Education and Social Policy and Institute for Policy Research also provided extensive support for the project, as did a group of colleagues who provided invaluable critique on the research. I am also grateful to the New Zealand Fulbright Committee for supporting my visit to New Zealand to discuss many of the ideas outlined in this book. I owe thanks to the Rockefeller Foundation for supporting a conference at Bellagio, where I was able to discuss and get feedback on this work from a wonderful group of scholars, and to the Carnegie Corporation (Grant # B 7615) for providing the resources to engage practitioners in conversations about the ideas outlined in the following pages. The National College of School Leadership in England supported numerous opportunities for conversations about school leadership, including the ILERN Network.

Many individuals—far too many to mention by name here—have contributed greatly to my thinking about distributed leadership over the past decade. I wish, however, to acknowledge the people who have taken the time to read and provide invaluable feedback on earlier drafts of this book or some part of it. This manuscript has benefited tremendously from the thoughtful critiques of Paul Cobb, David Cohen, Larry Cuban, Peter Gronn, Alma Harris, Fred Hess, Barton Hirsch, Gabrielle Lacomski, Ben Levin, Cecil Miskel, Enrique Orlina, Andrew Ortony, and Camille Rutherford. I owe a very special thank you to Andy Hargreaves, whose careful and incisive feedback on numerous versions helped push my thinking and writing. I thank Aditi Mohan, Marilyn Sherman, and Mark Swindle for their help and patience with editing, figures, and references.

As always, my immediate and extended family have provided unwavering love and support, for which I am greatly indebted to them. Finally, without the companionship and support of my partner Richard Czuba, this book would never have been written. He has been a tough critic of the work, endured all the headaches that come with such a writing project, and has done all this with grace and patience.

Of course, none of these individuals or agencies are responsible for the pages that follow. I alone take that responsibility.

J.P.S.

For Richard

The Author

James P. Spillane is the Spencer T. and Ann W. Olin Chair in Learning and Organizational Change at Northwestern University, professor of human development and social policy, professor of learning sciences, and faculty fellow at the Institute for Policy Research. He was formerly a primary school teacher in Ireland. Spillane's research focuses on local implementation of government education policy and on school leadership. He is author of *Standards Deviation: How Schools Misunderstand Education Policy* (2004) and numerous journal articles.

Distributed
Leadership

1

The Nature of the Beast

Setting the Scene

Adams School on Chicago's South Side is something of a success story. Serving students from homes well below the poverty line, Adams was in crisis in the late 1980s; only 16 percent of its students scored at or above national norms on standardized tests in reading. A decade later, administrators, teachers, and students at Adams had reason to celebrate. Students had made impressive gains on achievement tests, and attendance rates had improved considerably. Adams had developed a reputation as a success and as a place where teachers wanted to work.

As teachers and administrators at Adams tell the story, things began to change in 1988 when Brenda Williams took over the position of school principal. An assistant principal vividly recalled, "I could remember the very first day that she came in and we had a meeting . . . and it was a meeting that set forth her goal to come here and to make sure that academically we were growing . . . and she set before us the challenge that we have." Williams, an energetic African American woman, worked diligently during the 1990s to improve teaching and learning at Adams School. In local commentators', scholars', and teachers' telling of the Adams story, Williams gets much of the credit.

The Lure of Leaders in the "Heroics of Leadership" Genre

The Adams story will ring true for consumers of education literature the world over. It is a familiar tale: a charismatic principal takes
the helm in a failing school, setting new expectations for students
and staff alike and establishing new organizational routines and
structures in an effort to make over the school culture. Over time,
the principal's actions contribute to greater teacher satisfaction,
higher and shared expectations for student learning among staff,
and improved student achievement. Evidence of success begins to
accumulate as teachers report greater job satisfaction and higher
expectations for student learning.

Deservedly, principals like Williams become the stars of the education world, and their heroic acts become blueprints for "successful" school leadership. The success of these heroes and heroines
becomes the subject of academic publications, popular media
accounts, education folklore, and even an occasional documentary
or movie. In the "heroics of leadership" genre, or the "heroic leader
paradigm" (Yukl, 1999, p. 292), charismatic leaders and their gallant acts are center stage; everyone and everything else are at best
cast in minor, supporting roles. Even when others are cast in prominent roles, the focus is on the heroic actions of each individual, and
by adding together their individual efforts, one gets an account of
leadership. Letting go of the myth of individualism is difficult even
when leadership tales venture beyond the single hero or heroine to
acknowledge the part played by two or more supporting players.

A Distributed Perspective on Leadership: Essential Elements

In this book, I develop a distributed perspective on leadership as an
alternative to accounts that equate leadership with the gallant acts
of one or more leaders in an organization. My question is this: What

does it mean to take a distributed perspective on school leadership? A distributed leadership perspective moves beyond the Superman and Wonder Woman view of school leadership. It is about more than accounting for all the leaders in a school and counting up their various actions to arrive at some more comprehensive account of leadership. Moving beyond the principal or head teacher to include other potential leaders is just the tip of the iceberg, from a distributed perspective.

A distributed perspective is first and foremost about leadership practice (see Figure 1.1). This practice is framed in a very particular way, as a product of the joint interactions of school *leaders, followers,* and aspects of their *situation* such as tools and routines. This distributed view of leadership shifts focus from school principals like Brenda Williams and other formal and informal leaders to the web of leaders, followers, and their situations that gives form to leadership practice.

Distributed leadership means more than shared leadership. Too frequently, discussions of distributed leadership end prematurely with an acknowledgment that multiple individuals take responsibility for leadership: that there is a leader *plus* other leaders at work in the school. Though essential, this *leader-plus* aspect is not sufficient to

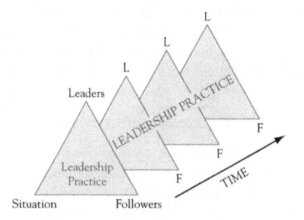

Figure 1.1. Leadership Practice from a Distributed Perspective.

capture the complexity of the practice of leadership. From a distributed perspective, it is the collective *interactions* among leaders, followers, and their situation that are paramount. The situation of leadership isn't just the context within which leadership practice unfolds; it is a defining element of leadership practice. Aspects of a situation—such as the Breakfast Club or the Five-Week Assessment routine at Adams School or a tool like student test data—don't simply affect or influence what school leaders do, enabling them to practice more or less effectively. These routines and tools are also produced by leadership practice. They mutually constitute leadership practice in interaction with leaders and followers.

In a distributed perspective on leadership, three elements are essential:

- Leadership *practice* is the central and anchoring concern.

- Leadership practice is generated in the *interactions* of leaders, followers, and their situation; each element is essential for leadership practice.

- The *situation* both defines leadership practice and is defined through leadership practice.

From a distributed perspective, leadership involves mortals as well as heroes. It involves the many and not just the few. It is about leadership practice, not simply roles and positions. And leadership practice is about interactions, not just the actions of heroes.

Problems with the Heroics of Leadership

The heroics of leadership genre is problematic for four reasons. First, heroic epics typically equate school leadership with school principals and their valiant actions. While other leaders are sometimes featured in these accounts, they are usually cast in minor, supporting roles. Vital though the school principal is, school leadership does not begin and end with the person in the principal's office.

Second, most accounts of school leadership pay scant attention to the *practice* of leadership (Hallinger and Heck, 1996). They dwell mostly on people, structures, functions, routines, and roles. And they focus on the "what" rather than the "how" of leadership, short-changing how leadership gets done through the ordinary, everyday practices involved in leadership routines and functions. While knowing *what* leaders do is important, knowing *how* they do it is also essential in understanding the practice of leadership. For example, recent scholarship implies that school leaders cultivate collaborative culture among teachers (an organizational function that is thought to be critical for school improvement) by setting tasks that involve teachers' working together (Goldring and Rallis, 1993; Liberman, Falk, and Alexander, 1994; Louis, Marks, and Kruse, 1996). Understanding *how* leadership practice creates these tasks in the day-to-day work of schools is as important as understanding what strategies help address which functions.

Third, when leadership practice does make it onto the radar screen, it is depicted mostly in terms of the actions, great or otherwise, of one or more leaders. Concentrating on individual actions fails to capture the significance of interactions.

Fourth, in the heroic leadership tradition, leadership is defined chiefly in terms of its outcome. This is problematic because leadership can occur without evidence of its outcome.

Fixating on the Heroic Leader

In many accounts of school leadership, the heroic leadership genre persists, with the school principal or head teacher as the protagonist, sometimes accompanied by assistant principals and others in formal leadership positions. Describing improvements at Adams School in this way is problematic because Brenda Williams did not turn the school around single-handedly. An array of other individuals—other administrators, specialists, and classroom teachers—with tools and routines of various hues were also critical in Adams makeover.

Williams is no slouch; she deserves to be the central character in the story of Adams's transformation. Yet, as in any good epic, what she did and how she did it depended in good measure on many others, who, by virtue of their formal roles or informal responsibilities, helped lead improvement efforts. Williams acknowledged the crucial role of others when she said, "I just couldn't do it all." She explained that she had put in place a group of leaders to help her transform Adams School. She reported, for example, that hiring an assistant to handle student disciplinary matters was critical: "I couldn't get involved in that day-to-day discipline and focus in on the instruction program too." A teacher at Adams also points to the importance of others in leading the transformation, remarking, "Starting with Dr. Williams . . . we have a very good team here. If they weren't who they are, we wouldn't be who we are. If the administration had not set the tone, we would not have adopted this tone." It was a team of people, albeit with Williams at the helm, that was critical in Adams School's transformation. Other administrators and classroom teachers took pivotal roles in leading efforts to improve instruction, transform school culture, and change the expectations that staff had for students. Some of these individuals simply did what they were told when Williams delegated responsibilities to them. Others rose to the occasion afforded by a new organizational culture and new organizational arrangements at Adams and took on leadership responsibilities. While Williams figures prominently in any account of leadership at Adams, she doesn't figure alone. Acknowledging that leadership practice extends beyond the school principal in no way undermines the vital role of the principal in school leadership but instead shows that leadership is often a collective rather than individualistic endeavor.

This first problem with the heroic leadership genre is addressed relatively easily by attending to the work of multiple leaders. I refer to this strategy as a *leader-plus* approach.

At Adams, for example, over a ten-year period, Williams and her staff worked on various organizational functions: constructing an instructional vision, developing teacher knowledge, procuring resources, and building a professional community. Further, Williams and her staff also constructed and institutionalized at Adams a number of leadership routines and structures in order to execute key organizational functions. These routines and structures included the School Improvement Planning Process, the Breakfast Club, and the Five-Week Assessment process. The Breakfast Club routine, a monthly meeting of teachers designed by school leaders to provide opportunities for teacher professional development, evolved over time as an opportunity to build professional community among teachers. A leader-plus approach recognizes that such routines and structures play an integral role in leadership.

Inattention to Leadership Practice

A few years ago, when I was describing leadership functions and arguing their importance for school improvement to a school principal, the principal retorted, "I know all that. Tell me how!" Understanding how leadership actually gets done in schools is imperative if research is to generate usable knowledge for school leaders. Describing the "what" is necessary but not sufficient to capture leadership practice.

Accounts of leadership often dwell exclusively on the structures and roles that schools should put in place and the leadership functions that need attention. The result is that day-to-day practice falls through the cracks. Studying the "how" as well as the "what" of leadership is essential.

An Incomplete Conception of Practice

Leadership practice is often equated with the actions of individuals. Practice writ large is thought about mostly in terms of the actions of the individual doing the practice. Hence, good or not-so-good practice is attributed almost entirely to the knowledge and skill of the individual practitioner. The elegance of the armoire is put down to the carpenter's skill and experience; the carpenter's tools rarely figure in the equation. But any skilled carpenter will tell you that the tools make a lot of difference in putting the armoire together. When it comes to practices of human improvement—teaching, leadership, psychotherapy—the situations are even more complex because practitioners often work in collectives and more often than not depend on their clients—students, followers, patients—to accomplish a task or implement some vision or goal. Hence, the practice of constructing and selling a vision for instructional improvement in a school cannot be understood by focusing solely on the actions of the school principal. For example, the practice of building and selling a new vision for instruction at Adams School had to do with more than the actions of Williams; this practice unfolded in the interactions among Williams and other leaders—assistant principals, literacy coordinators, teacher leaders—and in the interactions between leaders and followers. Further, the practice was enabled and constrained by an array of committees, routines, and tools, including student assessment instruments, regular staff get-togethers, and scheduling arrangements. These aspects of the situation often are ignored in attempts to account for leadership practice that fixate on the individual who is thought to be doing the practice. When tools and other aspects of the situation do figure in, they are seen as accessories to practice rather than essential, defining elements of it. Thinking about leadership in terms of interactions rather than actions offers a distinctly different perspective on leadership practice. Actions are still important, but they must be understood as part of interactions.

A Normative Definition of Leadership

One can point to Williams as a case of leadership because there is evidence that what she did influenced teachers' motivation, knowledge, and behavior, which in turn contributed to improvement in student outcomes at Adams School. Defining leadership like this is problematic because the existence of leadership is only acknowledged when there is evidence of its effects or effectiveness.

By way of illustration, consider Kosten School on Chicago's Northwest Side. At Kosten, a new principal and assistant principal worked to initiate routines designed to transform business as usual at the school, where teachers basically closed their doors and taught as they saw fit, with no oversight. The principal's and assistant principal's efforts to lead improvement in classroom instruction included regular reviews of teachers' grade books, monitoring of classroom instruction, and attention to following lesson plans. For some teachers, these efforts didn't influence their knowledge, motivation, or practice. But the motivation and practice of some teachers at Kosten were influenced by these collective endeavors, even if the effect was not universal. Even those teachers who openly resisted the improvement efforts understood them as leadership—practices designed to influence their work practices. Thus, relying on leadership outcomes—in particular, positive leadership outcomes—to infer the existence of leadership is problematic.

Defining leadership by relying on evidence of its outcomes or effects is not satisfactory because such definitions concentrate on a subset of what is considered to be leadership in organizations. Moreover, when leadership is defined chiefly in terms of its outcomes, efforts to study relationships between leadership and the effects of leadership end up as circular arguments. The distributed perspective addresses these shortcomings of the heroic leadership genre.

Prescription or Perspective?

Distributed leadership is frequently talked about as a cure-all for schools, a way that leadership ought to be carried out. But a distributed perspective on leadership should first be just that—a perspective or lens for thinking about leadership before rushing to normative action. In this view, distributed leadership is not a blueprint for doing school leadership more effectively. It is a way to generate insights into how leadership can be practiced more or less effectively.

A distributed perspective on leadership is best thought of as a framework for thinking about and analyzing leadership. It's a tool for helping us think about leadership in new and unfamiliar ways. It can be used as a frame to help researchers decide what to look at when they investigate leadership. A distributed perspective can be used as a diagnostic instrument that draws practitioners' and interventionists' attention to hidden dimensions of school leadership and helps practitioners approach their work in new ways. And it can be a way to acknowledge and perhaps even celebrate the many kinds of unglamorous and unheroic leadership that often go unnoticed in schools.

A distributed perspective on leadership is neither friend nor foe. It is not a prescription for better leadership but a description of how leadership already is. A distributed perspective might be a means to prescription, but it is not a prescription in itself.

What Is Leadership?

Over time, leadership has been defined in numerous ways. Perspectives on leadership have focused on group processes, personality and its effects, the exercise of influence; leadership has been seen as an act or behavior, a form of persuasion, and a power relation (Bass, 1990, p. 11). Bass (1990) defines leadership as "the interaction between two or more members of a group that often involves a structuring or restructuring of the situation and the perceptions and expectations of the members. Leaders are agents of change—persons whose acts affect other people more than other people's acts affect them. Leadership occurs when one group member modifies the motivation or competencies of others in the group" (pp. 19–20). Leadership thus is defined as a relationship of social influence.

One problem with definitions of this sort is that there is a tendency to define leadership in terms of its effectiveness or outcome; it is evident only when someone has been influenced, when someone's competency or motivation has been modified. However, as evidenced at Kosten School, teachers are not always influenced by the efforts of their principals and assistant principals to transform the status quo. Yet even teachers who ignore the guidance and motivation offered through leadership practice can see that these leadership practices are designed to influence their work. People can perceive activities as leadership even if they are not influenced by the activities. They do not rely on evidence of student learning to define the existence of teaching practice. Teaching practice sometimes fails to produce student learning; nonetheless it is still teaching.

Another problem with many definitions of leadership is that they focus on positive outcomes. However, leadership needn't necessarily involve outcomes or processes that are positive or beneficial. Leadership can influence people and organizations—indeed, entire societies—in directions that are not at all beneficial. Notorious figures such as Adolf Hitler practiced leadership effectively, but few would agree with the direction of his leadership. Teaching sometimes contributes to learning that most of us would not deem desirable—for example, when a dealer teaches teenagers how to traffic drugs. Nonetheless, it is still teaching. If leadership was determined only in terms of its outcomes and the desirability of such outcomes, why would one need to use qualifiers like *effective* and *ineffective* in discussing leadership?

Questions of effectiveness and direction of influence must be separated from leadership itself. *Leadership* refers to activities tied to the core work of the organization that are designed by organizational members to influence the motivation, knowledge, affect, or practices of other organizational members or that are understood by organizational members as intended to influence their motivation, knowledge, affect, or practices. Influence relationships that are not tied to the core work of the organization, such as one teacher influencing another to join Weight Watchers, would not count as leadership in this definition. Not all influence relations are ones of leadership; to denote leadership, the object of influence needs to be tied to the core work of the organization. The term *leadership* is reserved either for activities that administrators and teachers design to influence others or for activities that administrators, teachers, or students understand as influencing them, all in the service of the organization's core work. While leadership is frequently designed to initiate change, it can also be about preserving the status quo (Cuban, 1988) or even resisting change efforts.

Building a Framework for Seeing Things Anew

A distributed perspective on leadership involves two aspects: the leader-plus aspect and the practice aspect. While the leader-plus aspect is vital, it is insufficient on its own. The leadership practice aspect moves the focus from aggregating the actions of individual leaders to the interactions among leaders, followers, and their situation.

The Leader-Plus Aspect

A distributed perspective on leadership suggests that leadership doesn't reside in the principal's office any more than it does in the chief executive or the corner office of a multinational corporation. While corporate giants such as Bill Gates at Microsoft are often credited with building or turning around their companies, David Heenan and Warren Bennis show that these corporate giants rely on co-leaders—for instance, Steve Ballmer, in the case of Microsoft (Heenan and Bennis, 1999). Throughout history, from corporate boardrooms to Chairman Mao's China, those at the helm relied on partnerships with a trusted other to execute leadership; co-leadership was the modus operandi (Heenan and Bennis, 1999).

A distributed view of leadership also recognizes that leading schools requires multiple leaders. Occasionally, this may involve co-principals who share or divide up responsibility for running a school (Gronn, 2003; Grubb, Flessa, Tredway, and Stern, 2003). Moreover, from a distributed perspective, leadership is more than what individuals in formal leadership positions do. People in formal and informal roles take responsibility for leadership activities.

In addition to the principal, other potential school leaders include assistant principals, curriculum or subject specialists, and reading or Title 1 teachers. Individually or collectively, teachers take on leadership responsibilities, including mentoring peers and providing professional development. At Adams School, four teachers, all of whom have full-time teaching duties, take responsibility for many of the leadership tasks related to mathematics instruction.

Distribution of school leadership responsibilities across leaders does not arise solely through public decrees or private decisions of school administrators. Distributed leadership isn't just delegated leadership. Others, such as teachers and parents, take on leadership responsibility in schools on their own initiative. At one level, then, a distributed leadership perspective attempts to acknowledge and incorporate the work of all the individuals who have a hand in leadership practice. It presses us to examine who does what in the work of leadership. One strategy here might be to examine who is responsible for the functions that are thought to be essential for school improvement, including constructing and selling an instructional vision, building norms of trust and collaboration among staff, and supporting teacher development (Heller and Firestone, 1995).

The leader-plus perspective is an important component of a distributed framework, but it provides only part of what it means to take a distributed perspective on leadership. Adding in and adding up those responsible for leadership functions and activities in a school, while essential, is insufficient from a distributed perspective.

The Leadership Practice Aspect

The distributed leadership framework developed in this book pushes one step further than the leader-plus approach: it focuses attention on leadership practice, not just on leadership roles and functions and those who take responsibility for them. Leadership practice that takes shape in the interaction of leaders, followers, and their situation is central (see Figure 1.1).

Arguing that an "action perspective sees the reality of management as a matter of actions," Eccles and Nohria (1992, p. 13) encourage an approach to studying leadership that focuses on action rather than exclusively on structures, states, and designs. Defining leadership as activity allows for leadership from various positions in an organization (Heifetz, 1994) and puts the activity at the forefront, which is critical because "the strength of leadership as an influencing relation rests upon its effectiveness as activity" (Tucker, 1981, p. 25). In education, Heck and Hallinger (1999) argue that in-depth analysis of leadership practice is rare but essential if we are to make progress in understanding school leadership.

Most work that addresses leadership practice tends to equate it with the acts or actions of leaders. Frameworks for studying leadership practice are scarce, and they tend to privilege individual actions. Instead, from a distributed perspective, leadership practice takes shape in the interaction of leaders, followers, and their situation (Gronn, 2000; Spillane, Halverson, and Diamond, 2001, 2004). It is stretched over individuals who have responsibility for leadership routines. Further, these three elements in interaction mutually constitute leadership practice. Hence, in Figure 1.1, leadership practice is represented by a triangle, with each angle representing one of the three essential elements. While a single triangle represents the interactions among leaders, followers, and situation at a particular moment in time, the performance of a leadership routine involves multiple interactions. The multiple triangles in Figure 1.1 represent these interactions and underscore the importance of time. The broken lines connecting the triangles denote that over time (be it over the course of a twenty-minute faculty meeting or faculty meetings throughout a year), interactions can be more or less connected with one another.

The critical issue, then, is not whether leadership is distributed but how leadership is distributed. In this way, a distributed perspective presses us to investigate how leadership practice is stretched over two or more leaders and to examine how followers and the situation mutually constitute this practice.

I consider how leadership is stretched over leaders and then look at followers and the situation. My account is based on a multiyear study of school leadership that was carried out by me and my colleagues at Northwestern University, beginning in 1999, and that involved fifteen K–5 and K–8 schools in the Chicago area (The Distributed Leadership Study). This theory-building study employed mixed methods, including ethnography, structured observations, structured and semistructured interviews, teacher and principal questionnaires, social network surveys, and videos of leadership activities in schools. We used these methods over five years to build an understanding of leadership as a distributed practice.

Leaders and Leadership Practice

In a distributed leadership perspective, leadership practice is stretched over multiple leaders. Many of the leadership activities that my colleagues and I have observed in the Distributed Leadership Study are co-enacted. Both their design or initiation and their execution over time depend on the practices of two or more leaders. The design and initiation of the Breakfast Club at Adams involved multiple leaders. Its execution over time involved some of these same leaders as well as others, especially teacher leaders. Supporting teacher development through regular in-house professional development meetings is a common leadership activity in many of the schools we studied. Professional development in literacy education, for example, typically involves at least the principal, a literacy coordinator, and one or more teacher leaders working together. Sometimes the leaders' roles differ; at other times, their roles overlap. These leaders practice together, co-facilitating the professional development meetings. One leader steers the discussion, moderating input from participants, while another leader records participants' ideas. Another leader probes participants in an effort to clarify ideas and also works to build consensus in the group. Still another leader works on consensus building by restating core ideas and asking participants whether they agree while simultaneously reminding participants to focus on the big picture.

The leadership practice in these situations is stretched over all of the leaders that were described. Indeed, it might be best described as "in between" them.[1] The leadership practice takes form in the interactions among them. Leaders play off of and play into one another. What a leader does influences and in turn is influenced by other leaders. In this situation, leadership practice is a system of interacting practices that is more than the sum of the actions of individual leaders. A distributed perspective involves examining how leadership practice takes shape in the interactions among the practices of these leaders. Leadership is a system of practice made up of a collection of interacting component parts in relationships of interdependence in which the group has distinct properties over and above the individuals who make it up. I will return to these issues in Chapter Three.

Consider the performance of a dance such as a two-step. While the individual actions of partner 1 and partner 2 are essential, the performance of the two-step takes place in the interactions of the partners. Hence, the practice of the two-step is *in between* the two partners. An account of the actions of each partner fails to capture the practice; it is essential to analyze the interactions. Moreover, the music—an important aspect of the situation—is essential in defining the practice, providing the rhythm for four steps to six beats. Indeed, one could also argue that the practice of the two-step is in between the two partners and the music.

Working together is sufficient but not necessary: while school leaders sometimes work together, at other times, they work separately yet interdependently. At Ellis School on Chicago's West Side, for example, the principal and assistant principal both monitor and evaluate classroom teaching, a core leadership function in their efforts to improve instruction. Thus, monitoring instruction at Ellis is stretched over the separate practices of the two leaders, and it is in the interaction of these two component parts that leadership practice takes shape over the course of a school year. I will return to this example in Chapter Three.

Followers and Leadership Practice

The follower dimension is another essential component of leadership practice. Classroom teachers, administrators, specialists, and others can, depending on the leadership activity, find themselves in the follower role. In using the term *follower*, I merely wish to distinguish those in leader roles from others involved in a leadership routine. Leaders not only influence followers but are also influenced by them (Dahl, 1961; Cuban, 1988). A distributed perspective on leadership not only acknowledges the centrality of followers to leadership but also casts followers in a new light, as an essential element that mutually constitutes leadership practice. Thus, leadership is not simply something that is done to followers; followers in interaction with leaders and the situation contribute to defining leadership practice. Observing leadership practice in schools, I am struck by the role that followers play in defining the nature of that practice.

Situation and Leadership Practice

Leaders work in interaction not just with followers but also with aspects of the situation, including routines and tools. School leaders, like the rest of us, do not work directly on the world; they work with various aspects of their situation.

Routines are taken for granted as a part of daily life. They involve everything from getting to work in the morning to teaching a reading lesson. Routines involve two or more actors in "a repetitive, recognizable pattern of interdependent actions" (Feldman and

Pentland, 2003, p. 96). Consider the Five-Week Assessment routine at Adams School, an activity that is repeated every five weeks and that everyone at Adams recognizes. The routine involves seven interdependent steps, including creating the student assessment instrument, scoring and analyzing students' responses, and determining instructional strategies to address problems identified by the assessment. This routine engages multiple parties, from the literacy coordinator to the school principal. Routines are part and parcel of life in schools.

Tools are externalized representations of ideas that are used by people in their practice (Norman, 1988; Wertsch, 1998). Tools include student assessment data, observation protocols for evaluating teachers, lesson plans, and student academic work. These tools mediate how people practice, shaping interactions among leaders and followers in particular ways.

In my research in schools, I find it impossible to describe leadership practice without referring to all sorts of tools, including observation protocols, students' work, student test score data, and various organizational structures. Yet tools do not figure prominently in most accounts of school leadership, in part because leadership practice has not been a central focus in such work. When they do, they are usually treated as accessories to leadership practice, things that allow individuals to practice more efficiently, and leadership practice is considered to be entirely a result of the skill and knowledge of the practitioner. Thinking of tools as accessories that simply allow leaders to practice more or less efficiently misses the fact that tools in interaction with leaders and followers fundamentally shape the practice. For example, the Internet as a tool fundamentally transforms how most of us do a lot of common chores—for instance, shopping for books, finding telephone numbers, making airline reservations, or checking in for flights. In some respects, the Internet enables us to perform some of these tasks more efficiently. But the Internet also fundamentally changes the practice of checking in for a flight or purchasing a book. In the Internet age, purchasing a book does not require direct interaction with another individual; with the click of a mouse, one can see what other customers thought about the book under consideration or access a host of related titles. The Internet doesn't just make buying a book more or less efficient; it changes how that purchasing practice is performed.

From a distributed perspective, tools and routines are an integral element that constitutes leadership practice. Other aspects of the situation—for instance, committee structures and organizational culture—are also important but are beyond the scope of this book. I confine my discussion to tools and routines. Relationships between tools and routines and leadership practice are likely to hold for other aspects of the situation.

Taking a distributed perspective involves more than simply acknowledging the importance of tools, routines, and structures to the leadership enterprise and then identifying which tools figure in which leadership practices. A distributed perspective necessitates understanding *how* aspects of the situation enable and constrain that practice and thereby contribute to defining it. Brenda Williams related that when she took over as principal at Adams School, one of her initial tasks was to build an infrastructure that would enable a new sort of leadership practice for teaching and learning. To build professional community among her staff and promote teacher development, Williams and her colleagues created the Breakfast Club routine, a regular morning meeting in which teachers discussed research about teaching and learning. To monitor teaching and learning and identify areas for improvement, Williams and her colleagues created the Five-Week Assessment routine. She explained, "We felt it was important to have a structure within our school so that we would know on a regular basis, on an ongoing basis, if our students were mastering the concepts." These routines, as I will discuss in Chapter Three, contributed to defining leadership practice at Adams School.

While tools and other aspects of a situation contribute to defining leadership practice, they can also be redefined through that practice. Tools and routines do not straitjacket leadership practice. Instead, tools and routines are made and remade in and through leadership practice; their genesis is in leadership practice. For example, Williams and her leadership team at Adams inherited a school in which the organizational infrastructure privatized classroom practice and did not encourage dialogue among teachers. Together with her colleagues, Williams worked to change this infrastructure, breaking down the school's "egg carton" structure (Lortie, 1975) and creating opportunities for teachers to talk about their teaching. This new infrastructure in turn shaped leadership practice at Adams. Organizational routines and tools are bundles of possibilities that shape leadership practice but can also be reshaped by that practice. Tools and routines can be made, remade, and reappropriated for purposes for which they were not originally intended.

Distributed Leadership: A Case of Old Wine in New Bottles?

Some people wonder what is new about a distributed leadership perspective. Does the emperor have any new clothes? This depends on the particular definition of distributed leadership to which one subscribes. Some people see distributed leadership as a replica rather than a relative of other leadership constructs and approaches.

Scholars of leadership have long argued for the need to move beyond those at the top of organizations in order to examine leadership (Katz and Kahn, 1966; Barnard, 1938). Savvy critics have argued for paying attention to the shifting coalitions of decision makers in organizations in order to understand leadership (Cyert and March, 1963; March and Olsen, 1984). Research on schools has generated evidence that the school principal does not have a monopoly on school leadership; teachers, administrators, and other professionals also play important leadership roles (Smylie and Denny, 1990). In light of this literature, the leader-plus aspect of a distributed framework is in some respects a case of old wine in new bottles: it involves relabeling a familiar phenomenon.

Still, recent work has generated some important and new insights into the leader-plus aspect of distributed leadership, and I will consider these in Chapter Two. Moreover, while scholars may have long argued that leadership extends beyond those at the top of an organization, often their teachings appear to fall on deaf ears; both empirical research and development work on school leadership continue to focus chiefly on the school principal. Indeed, the effective schools literature has helped to continue the tradition of equating school leadership with the principal. School principals are very important to school leadership, but their importance is not such that school principals and school leadership are one and the same. Hence, while the leader-plus aspect of distributed leadership may not represent a radical extension of the existing knowledge base, it is a crucial aspect nonetheless.

One response to the prevalence of the "view from the top" has been to focus attention on teacher leadership. However, the tendency to compartmentalize school leadership by creating pigeonholes for principal leadership and teacher leadership also has its problems—for instance, a disjointed portrayal of leadership resulting from the fact that interrelationships between teacher leadership and administrator leadership are rarely discussed. Relatively little is known about how leadership practice is stretched over formal leaders and teacher leaders. A distributed perspective urges us to take leadership practice as the unit of interest and attend to both teachers as leaders and administrators as leaders simultaneously. By placing investigations of teacher leadership in the context of leadership practice, a distributed perspective recognizes something old and adds something new.

In its treatment of both the situation of leadership and the role of followers in leadership, distributed leadership blends old ideas with new ones. Like prior leadership research, the distributed perspective takes the situation seriously. Contingency theorists have long argued that aspects of the situation, such as school size, influence what leaders do and mediate their effects on teachers (Fiedler, 1973; Bossert, Dwyer, Rowan, and Lee, 1982; Murphy, 1991). While still acknowledging the importance of the situation, a distributed perspective treats the situation differently from prior work. From a distributed view, the situation is not simply a context within which school leaders practice; it is a defining element of practice. The situation—tools and routines of various sorts—shapes leadership from the inside out rather than from the outside in. Distributed leadership views the situation in interaction with leaders and followers as an element that mutually constitutes leadership practice. In this view, the situation does not simply affect what school leaders do; in interaction with leaders and followers, the situation defines leadership practice.

The distributed perspective also affords followers a prominent place in discussions of leadership practice. In this respect, the distributed leadership perspective concurs with research that suggests that leaders depend on followers to lead (Dahl, 1961; Hollander, 1978; Cuban, 1988). A distributed perspective on leadership extends this work by casting followers as an essential constituting element in defining leadership activity. Like the situation, followers are seen as a defining element of leadership activity, shaping it from the inside out rather than from the outside in. In this way, the distributed perspective positions followers differently with respect to leadership practice and thus departs from prior scholarship.

Replica or Relative?

People frequently use the terms *collaborative leadership, shared leadership, co-leadership, democratic leadership, situational leadership,* and *distributed leadership* interchangeably. Sometimes distributed leadership is discussed as though it were the same as or a type of transformational leadership. From my point of view, this is wrong; they are not synonyms. A distributed perspective on leadership is a relative, not a replica of these constructs or approaches.

While collaborative leadership is by definition distributed, all distributed leadership is not necessarily collaborative. Indeed, a distributed perspective allows for leadership that can be more collaborative or less collaborative, depending on the situation. At Kosten School, where the principal and assistant principal worked to transform classroom teaching, a group of veteran teachers worked to preserve the status quo. Although the leadership in this situation can be understood from a distributed perspective, it is not collaborative; school administrators tugged in one direction, while veteran teachers pulled in the opposite direction. Similarly, a distributed perspective on leadership allows for democratic leadership or autocratic leadership. From a distributed perspective, leadership can be stretched over leaders in a school but not necessarily democratically (Wood, 2004). For example, the leadership practice in mathematics at Adams is rather autocratic compared with that in language arts. Leadership practice for mathematics typically involves the teacher leaders doing most of the talking, telling teachers about resources and teaching strategies. In contrast, leadership practice for literacy involves much more back-and-forth between leaders and teachers as they work together to construct teaching strategies. However, even though it is more autocratic, mathematics leadership practice at Adams is still distributed in that it is defined in the interactions of leaders, followers, and situation. Similarly, studying team leadership does not necessarily involve taking a distributed perspective. One can adopt a team leadership approach without ever attending to leadership practice. Moreover, practice can be viewed simply as a function of the team rather than as a function of the interaction of leaders, followers, and the situation.

Co-leadership reflects a distribution of leadership, but the distributed perspective involves more, urging us to move beyond the leader-plus aspect to consider how leadership practice takes shape in the interaction of leaders, followers, and aspects of the situation.

Co-leadership, according to Heenan and Bennis (1999), happens when "power and responsibility are dispersed [among] . . . co-leaders with shared values and aspirations, all of whom work together toward common goals" (p. 5). The distributed perspective developed in this book differs from this view by focusing on practice and taking followers and the situation into account. Furthermore, co-leadership relies on the leaders having shared values, aspirations, and goals. From a distributed perspective, however, instances of practice in which the leaders do not have shared values and may be working on goals that are not identical are still distributed. Hence, not all distributed leadership is co-leadership.

Finally, let us consider the relationship between transformational leadership and distributed leadership.[2] While the literature provides no agreed-on definition of transformational leadership, it is typically contrasted with transactional leadership. Transformational leadership is usually defined as the "ability to empower others" with the purpose of bringing about a "major change in the form, nature, and function of some phenomenon" (Leithwood, Begley, and Cousins, 1992, p. 25; also Burns, 1978). Similarly, Bennis's (1959) notion of transformative leadership centers on the ability of a person to reach others in a fashion that raises their consciousness and inspires them to greatness. Understanding the needs of individual staff members is more important than trying to coordinate and control them. A transactional approach, in contrast, casts leader-follower interactions as a social exchange relationship: "you scratch my back, I'll scratch yours." In addition, in many accounts of transformational leadership, the heroics of leadership genre flourishes, with the school principal as the creator of all things good.

A distributed perspective on leadership differs conceptually from transformational leadership in at least two respects. First, a distributed perspective on leadership does not privilege a transformational perspective over a transactional one; from a distributed perspective, leadership can be either transformational or transactional. A distributed perspective on leadership is agnostic on the mechanisms of social influence used in leadership practice. Second, a distributed perspective on leadership puts leadership practice center stage rather than the chief executive or the principal; it allows for others—for instance, administrators or teachers—as key players in leadership practice either by design or by default.

Leadership Practice and Instruction

How does school leadership practice connect with its object—the core of schooling, teaching and learning? While teaching is typically thought of as a function of an individual teacher's knowledge, skills, and actions, teaching is actually a co-production, something that teachers and students do together with particular material (Cohen and Ball, 1998). Any experienced teacher will tell you that the same lesson can play out very differently from one year to the next, depending on the group of students involved. Students matter to teaching practice because teachers construct teaching in interaction with students. Teachers, students, and materials mutually constitute classroom instruction.

Thinking about instruction in this way has implications for understanding relationships between leadership practice and instructional practice. In exploring relationships between school leadership and teaching and learning, scholars often focus too narrowly on the connections between school leaders' work and teachers' classroom work. Leadership practice, however, might connect with teaching and learning practice through a variety of different activities that are linked directly to students, teachers, materials, or some combination of the three. So, in thinking about the relationship between leadership practice as a distributed practice and teaching and learning, one must examine how leadership activities connect with teachers and also how leadership activities connect with students and the materials that teachers and students work with. My research on distributed leadership suggests that some leadership activities connect with teaching and learning directly through students rather than exclusively or chiefly through teachers.

Conclusion

Leadership practice typically involves more than one person—if not by design, then by default and by necessity. It is difficult to imagine how things could be otherwise. Expecting one person to single-handedly lead efforts to improve instruction in a complex organization such as a school is impractical. Leadership is too often portrayed as a synonym for what the school principal or some other formal or informal leader does. Other sources of leadership in schools are ignored or treated as supplementary and important but almost always secondary to the real leadership that comes from the principal's office. A distributed perspective offers an alternative way of thinking about leadership in schools by foregrounding leadership practice and by suggesting that leadership practice is constructed in the interactions between leaders, followers, and their situations. While not a prescription for how to practice school leadership, distributed leadership offers a framework for thinking about leadership differently. As such, it enables us to think about a familiar phenomenon in new ways that come closer to approximating leadership on the ground than many of the conventional and popular recipes for school leadership.

In Chapter Two, I consider what is known about the leader-plus aspect of a distributed perspective, while in Chapter Three I consider what is known about the practice aspect of a distributed perspective. Chapter Four examines the strategic implications of a distributed perspective for leadership practice, policy, and school leader preparation and development.

Notes

1. I borrow the notion of "in between" from Salomon and Perkins (1998), who use it to discuss the notion of distributed expertise.

2. In my original articulation of the distributed leadership framework, I argued that my working definition of leadership was consistent with a transformational perspective on leadership. Based on my ongoing data analysis, however, I have modified this view considerably.

2

The Leader-Plus Aspect

Setting the Scene

It is early Tuesday morning at Baxter Elementary School on Chicago's Northwest Side. The literacy committee is in full swing in the school library. Down the hall in one of the sixth-grade classrooms, the mathematics committee is in session. Fueled by the principal's longitudinal analysis of student test data, which showed slumping student test scores in the middle grades, both of these leadership routines are designed to lead improvement in teaching and learning.

The school's literacy coordinators, the school librarian, and numerous teacher leaders lead the weekly literacy committee meetings, along with other leadership routines tied to literacy at Baxter. Chairing the literacy committee, for example, has rotated among the literacy coordinators and some teacher leaders. In addition, teachers readily take on leadership responsibilities for various tasks as the need arises or as opportunities present themselves. A sixth-grade teacher with a degree in mathematics was the chief mover and shaker in implementing the weekly mathematics committee meeting and other leadership routines for mathematics.

Weekly curricular subcommittee meetings are a staple at Baxter and are part of an elaborate infrastructure that is designed to support leadership for instruction and to engage teachers in that work.

Other leadership routines include bimonthly grade-level meetings and monthly faculty leadership group meetings, each implemented by a different combination of administrators, specialists, and teachers.

Overview

While distributed leadership may be a hot topic in education circles, empirical knowledge about it is thin. One recent review of the literature on distributed leadership conducted by scholars in the United Kingdom identified a limited empirical knowledge base (Bennett, Harvey, Wise, and Woods, 2003). We do not know a great deal about leadership from a distributed perspective, although we can infer a reasonable amount from research in other traditions. The barren empirical landscape is to be expected, given that ideas about distributed leadership are still in their infancy. Distributed leadership has garnered sustained attention from scholars, school reformers, and practitioners only over the past half decade, although the term entered the social science lexicon before that.

Most scholarship on distributed leadership, as one would expect, considering the novelty of the ideas, focuses on theory development and hypothesis generation, an important precursor to hypothesis-testing work. Figuring out the nature of the beast is imperative before measuring its effects on teaching and learning.

This chapter and the next center on the following question: What do we know about leadership from a distributed perspective? In this chapter, I focus chiefly on the leader-plus aspect, while in the next chapter, I take a closer look at the practice aspect.

If, according to a distributed perspective, school administrators do not have a monopoly on leadership, then it behooves us to examine the distribution of responsibility for leadership work. In the opening scenario, an array of administrators, specialists, and classroom teachers at Baxter Elementary School take responsibility for leadership work, although this work differs, depending on the routine and the subject area. Reviewing the literature and examining the evidence from my own research, I consider four questions in this chapter:

- Who takes responsibility for leadership work?

- How are these responsibilities arranged?

- How do these arrangements come to pass?

- How do individuals get constructed as influential leaders?

Who Performs Leadership Work?

Multiple individuals typically perform leadership work. Evidence suggests that in addition to school principals and assistant principals, other formally designated leaders and teachers take responsibility for leadership routines and functions. A recent study of more than one hundred U.S. elementary schools found that responsibility for leadership functions was typically distributed across three to seven formally designated leadership positions per elementary school (Camburn, Rowan, and Taylor, 2003). Such positions included principals; assistant principals; program coordinators or facilitators; subject area coordinators or facilitators; mentors, master teachers, or teacher consultants; and other "auxiliary" professional staff, such as family outreach workers. Defining leadership as a set of organizational functions rather than tying leadership to a particular administrative position, Heller and Firestone (1995) also found in a study of eight elementary schools that multiple leaders, including school district personnel and external consultants, were taking responsibility for leadership.

Some studies cast wider nets than others by looking beyond those in formally designated leadership positions. This work offers convincing evidence that teachers are also key in the performance of leadership functions and routines (Heller and Firestone, 1995; Spillane, Diamond, and Jita, 2003). Heller and Firestone found that while those with formally designated leadership positions performed some functions, individuals who had no formal leadership position also took responsibility for leadership functions. Teachers contributed to an array of leadership functions, including sustaining the program vision and informally monitoring program implementation (Heller and Firestone, 1995; Firestone, 1989).

Similarly, research on Australian schools (Crowther, Kaagan, Ferguson, and Hann, 2002) and U.S. and Canadian schools (Hargreaves and Fink, 2004) shows that teachers, on their own or collectively, take responsibility for leadership functions and routines, at times in an effort to make up for leadership gaps that result from formally designated leaders' lack of expertise or oversight. The case of rural Sunbeach Elementary and Middle School described by Crowther and his colleagues is illustrative. Energized by a professional development workshop on an integrated approach to literacy, Loretta, a learning support teacher at Sunbeach, took it upon herself to reform literacy instruction. Recognizing that she lacked positional authority, she enlisted the support of her principal, who encouraged her to share her ideas with the staff. Although Sunbeach's curriculum team expressed concerns at the outset, Loretta's commitment and enthusiasm, together with the respect she commanded from her colleagues, won the day. Over time, with help from the principal and one of her colleagues, Loretta enlisted teachers at Sunbeach in a revision of the school's literacy program (Crowther, Kaagan, Ferguson, and Hann, 2002).

Based on interviews conducted in a study of twenty-one schools in four U.S. cities, Portin and his colleagues also showed that responsibility for leadership is distributed not only among appointed leaders but also among de facto leaders—that is, individuals who, regardless of their position, exercise influence on others with respect to the direction the school is taking or should take (Portin, Schneider, DeArmond, and Gundlach, 2003). This study of elementary, middle, high, and K–12 schools showed that this pattern of distributed responsibility for leadership is not confined to elementary schools.

My work, which is part of the Distributed Leadership Study in thirteen Chicago K–5 and K–8 schools, also shows that leadership is distributed among those in formal leadership positions and teachers not in formal leadership positions. However, this work suggests that an exclusive focus on self-reports about the performance of leadership functions may distort the inferred distribution of responsibility. Analyzing the performance of leadership routines in schools, we found that many routines are designed to address or, over time, evolve to address various leadership functions. School leaders at Adams School developed the Breakfast Club routine to support teacher development and build professional community among staff. Similarly, school leaders designed the Five-Week Assessment routine to monitor instruction, and over time, it also became an important means of identifying teacher development needs at Adams. Any one leadership routine may serve various leadership functions. Furthermore, good intentions or the best-laid plans do not always find their way into practice. What actually happens in the observed daily performance of routines and what leaders report in interviews and surveys—the organization as lived as distinct from as designed— are not always mirror images of each other.

While leadership is distributed both among formally designated leaders and among those who are not formally designated as leaders, this does not mean that everyone in the school has a hand in every leadership function or routine. The distribution of leadership differs, depending on the leadership function or routine, the subject matter, the type of school, the school's size, and a school or school leadership team's developmental stage. I elaborate on each of these in the sections that follow.

Distribution Depends on Leadership Function

School principals and, to a lesser extent, assistant principals performed a broader range of functions, including instructional leadership functions, building management functions, and boundary spanning functions (for example, functions that focus on procuring resources or establishing and sustaining relationships with external constituents such as district office staff and parents), compared with occupants of other formally designated leadership positions (Camburn, Rowan, and Taylor, 2003). In contrast, coaches associated with the comprehensive school reform (CSR) models concentrated on instructional leadership, devoting less time to building management and boundary-spanning functions.[1] Thus, while the principal and assistant principal tended to be generalists in that they focused on instruction, building management, and boundary-spanning functions, individuals in CSR coach positions (that is, coach positions associated with a CSR model) and other formally designated leadership positions (for example, master teachers or subject area coordinators) tended to be specialists. CSR coaches, for example, prioritized work on instructional leadership functions over other leadership functions.

The distribution of responsibility for instructional leadership also differed by the particular function. While the CSR coaches put a premium on instructional capacity building, school principals reported giving priority to instructional goal setting and monitoring improvement (Camburn, Rowan, and Taylor, 2003). When district administrators got involved in school leadership, they tended to work on particular functions; district office staff typically were not involved in functions such as monitoring program implementation or handling disturbances (Heller and Firestone, 1995).

My own work as part of the Distributed Leadership Study shows similar patterns, suggesting that the range of distribution depends on the particular routine. Some routines, such as formative evaluations of classroom teaching and, to a lesser extent, informal monitoring of instruction, tend to involve no more than one or two leaders—typically, the principal and assistant principal. In contrast, performance of leadership routines such as teacher development typically involves more leaders and, in addition to formally designated leaders, typically involves teachers and individuals from outside the school. Teacher professional development in language arts instruction in all schools in our study usually involved the principal, assistant principal, another formally designated leader such as a literacy coordinator, a teacher leader, and often an external consultant or staff person from the district office.

Distribution Depends on Subject Matter

The distribution of leadership among formal leaders and teachers also depends on the subject matter (Spillane, Diamond, and Jita, 2003). Researchers in the Distributed Leadership Study found that the number of individuals involved in the performance of a leadership routine and the extent to which formally designated leaders were involved depended on the school subject. The performance of leadership routines such as professional development or curriculum development for language arts instruction typically involved more leaders—both formally designated leaders and teacher leaders—than similar leadership routines related to mathematics or science instruction. Two to five leaders, depending on the routine and the school, usually performed leadership routines for language arts. In contrast, two or three leaders carried out leadership routines for mathematics, whereas only one or two leaders took responsibility for leadership routines for science. School principals and assistant principals were more likely to be involved in the performance of leadership routines for language arts, less likely to be involved in leadership routines for mathematics, and even less likely to be involved in leadership routines for science.

The distribution of leadership, then, is partly a function of the subject area. Subject area differences result in part because school leaders prioritize subjects differently. For elementary school administrators and teachers, science is not nearly as high a priority as literacy or mathematics. But the different work norms that have evolved for different subject areas at both elementary and secondary school levels also contribute to differences in the distribution of leadership (Ball, 1981; Little, 1993; Siskin, 1994; Spillane, 2000; Stodolsky, 1988, 1989; Stodolsky and Grossman, 1995).

Distribution Depends on School Type

The distribution of responsibility for leadership functions and routines among formal leaders and teachers also appears to differ according to the type of school—public, private, charter, Catholic, or magnet school. Portin, Schneider, DeArmond, and Gundlach (2003), in their study of twenty-one U.S. schools, found that who takes responsibility depends in part on the type of school and the area in which leadership is being exercised. Arguing that regardless of the type of school, leadership is imperative in seven critical areas (instruction, culture, management, human resources, strategic planning, external development, and micropolitics), Portin and his colleagues found that responsibility for leadership in these areas differed depending on the type of school in which the leadership practice took place.

Leaders in private or entrepreneurial schools were more likely than public school leaders to report distributing responsibility for leadership in several critical leadership areas. Specifically, principals in private and entrepreneurial schools were more likely to distribute leadership in the areas of culture, strategic vision, and human resources. In some public schools, the district office was a player in human resources and instructional leadership, while in some private schools, managerial leadership was provided in part by school boards. While relationships between the type of school and the distribution of responsibility for leadership work are neither simple nor direct, the governance or policy system in which a school is nested does matter when it comes to school leadership arrangements.

Distribution Depends on School Size

School size appears to affect the distribution of leadership among formal leaders and teachers. A study of more than one hundred U.S. elementary schools found that, in general, the larger the school, the greater was the number of formally designated leaders over whom responsibility for leadership was distributed; larger schools had larger leadership teams (Camburn, Rowan and Taylor, 2003). This study, however, focused exclusively on formally designated leaders and did not include informal leadership—for example, teachers who take on leadership responsibilities. It is possible that larger schools would have more informal leadership than smaller schools due to the sheer volume of leadership work. Still, other factors, such as a school's developmental stage, are likely to influence the distribution of leadership among informal leaders.

Distribution Depends on Development Stage

A school's or school leadership team's developmental stage also appears to influence the distribution of leadership among formal leaders and teachers. Time is a key variable. Alma Harris's work on shared leadership in the United Kingdom suggests that time is important in understanding arrangements for performing leadership functions and routines. Specifically, head teachers adopted approaches for distributing leadership that were appropriate to where the school was along a developmental trajectory rather than relying on some static "ideal" leadership approach (Harris, 2002). As a school evolves through a change process, the distribution of leadership responsibility among its leaders changes.

Michael Copland underscores the notion that the distribution of leadership in schools shifts over time, with school leaders' roles evolving depending on where the school is in the improvement process. Copland's study involved eighty-six schools that were part of the Bay Area School Reform Collaborative (BASRC), a reform effort that was designed to reculture schools in order to enable whole-school change (Copland, 2004). BASRC's theory of change is built on ideas that acknowledge the importance of distribution and functional expertise in school leadership. Analyzing inquiry practices in these schools, Copland identified three possible stages of inquiry—novice, intermediate, and expert—and concluded that the distribution of leadership among formal leaders and teachers differed according to the school's stage. Early in reform work, formal leaders, especially the principal and BASRC coordinator, were critical in getting and keeping reform on the school's agenda. At this stage, leadership teams worked mainly as sounding boards for principals. Over time, new structures emerged to support the distribution of leadership among formal leaders and teachers, and in the process, leaders' roles were transformed; experience enabled people to perform more effectively in particular roles, which created opportunities for leadership to be distributed among others (Copland, 2004).

How Are Leadership Responsibilities Arranged?

Schools have different arrangements for distributing leadership among formal leaders and informal leaders. Distribution of responsibility for the performance of leadership functions and routines is not always analogous to either synchronized swimming or relay running. Some arrangements bear resemblance to relay running; many bear more resemblance to soccer or basketball.

The evidence suggests at least three arrangements:

- Division of labor

- Co-performance

- Parallel performance

Several types of arrangements can coexist in the same school, differing according to the leadership function or routine.

Division of Labor

A single leadership position rarely takes responsibility for a particular leadership function. Rather than a neat division of labor for
leadership work, leaders in different positions perform various leadership functions with considerable overlap among positions (Heller
and Firestone, 1995).

In the course of the Distributed Leadership Study, I found some
evidence of a division of labor with respect to certain leadership routines, especially teacher evaluation and student discipline. In many
schools, the assistant principal took primary responsibility for student discipline, ensuring an orderly and safe school environment—
an important leadership function. This was the case at Adams
School; Brenda Williams reported that early in her tenure as principal, she realized that she could not take responsibility for everything. Student discipline and student attendance were important
leadership functions in Williams's scheme of things but were functions that she could not address adequately if she wished to do a
good job of improving instruction, so she got other leaders at Adams
to work on them. Still, such arrangements were not the norm for
leadership work. Moreover, patterns varied across schools; for example, we found evidence of a school principal handling school discipline while hiring an assistant principal to take the lead on matters
of instruction. A neat division of labor with respect to leadership
work is not the standard operating procedure in schools. When it
does exist, predictable patterns are difficult to identify.

Co-Performance

A second arrangement involves two or more leaders performing a
leadership function or routine in a collaborated fashion. Thus, leadership is co-performed (Gronn, 2003; Spillane, Diamond, and Jita,
2003). In the Distributed Leadership Study, we found evidence of
co-performance for various leadership routines, including teacher

development, curriculum development, curricular material selection, and school improvement planning. Working together, formally designated leaders, teachers, and sometimes individuals from outside the school perform leadership routines or execute leadership functions (Heller and Firestone, 1995; Gronn, 2003).

Parallel Performance

Leaders don't always work in a collaborated manner; they often work in parallel to execute the same leadership functions or routines and, in so doing, duplicate one another's work. A third arrangement thus involves people performing the same functions or routines but without coordination among the various leaders. Leaders perform the same leadership work in parallel and redundantly, carrying out the same leadership function (Camburn, Rowan, and Taylor, 2003; Gronn, 2003; Heller and Firestone, 1995). Redundancy is not all bad; it has advantages. For example, having multiple leaders work, even in parallel, on selling the same instructional vision to school staff can help reinforce the vision and potentially increase the likelihood of buy-in on the part of teachers. Of course, when working in parallel, leaders can also serve different or even conflicting instructional visions.

Goals and Means in Leadership Arrangements

The three arrangements of leadership responsibility—division of labor, co-performance, and parallel performance—can involve leaders striving for similar goals but can also involve leaders striving for different or even conflicting goals as they take on responsibility for the same leadership routine. A leader or group of leaders in a school can push one instructional vision in a school, while another leader or group of leaders work in parallel to sell an altogether different vision for instruction. Hence, individuals can perform the same leadership routine but in ways that are intended to promote different or even contrary goals.

School leaders can push or pull in opposing directions. In the Distributed Leadership Study, this arrangement was most evident at Kosten School, where a new principal and assistant principal established new leadership routines that were designed to standardize content coverage and grading practices at the school (see Chapter One). Some veteran teachers at the school, however, were pulling in the opposite direction, working to maintain the status quo. While leadership work at this school was distributed among formal leaders and teachers, different leaders were pulling in opposing directions. The literature on schools and school change offers many vivid examples of leadership in opposition, in which formally designated leaders and teachers perform leadership routines that are intended to promote different or contradictory goals (Firestone, 1979).

Similarly, the strategies that leaders use or the roles they take on as they co-perform or work in parallel can also differ from one leader to the next. Different means, however, are not necessarily contrary. Take the good cop, bad cop situation. Both cops can have the same goal—to get the prisoner to confess—but adopt very different roles involving different strategies as they co-perform the interrogation. Similar situations are possible when two or more individuals work on the performance of the same leadership routine.

How Does Leadership Get Distributed?

Another issue concerns how different arrangements for the distribution of leadership come to pass in schools. The distribution of responsibility for leadership can result *by design* from the decisions of formal and informal leaders, either individually or collectively. The design decisions of individuals and agencies beyond the schoolhouse, including school districts and other external agents and agencies, can also influence the distribution of leadership. However, leadership distribution does not come to pass only through the public decrees or private decisions of leaders. The distribution of responsibility for leadership functions and routines can also result *by default* when formal leaders or teacher leaders, either individually or collectively, take on responsibility for some leadership routine or function. The distribution of leadership among leaders evolves over time as individuals get to know one another's skills and weaknesses, develop trust, and create working relationships that contribute to the distribution of leadership. Finally, the distribution of leadership can emerge *through crisis* when a school encounters an unanticipated problem or challenge and formal leaders and teachers find themselves working together to address it. These different mechanisms are not mutually exclusive; they work in tandem and in interaction.

Distribution of Leadership by Design

Through their design decisions, formally designated leaders and teachers together or on their own can influence the distribution of responsibility for the performance of leadership functions and routines in schools. This can happen in one of two ways. First, creating formally designated leadership positions or reframing existing positions can shape the distribution of leadership among formal leaders and teachers. Second, creating structures and routines that enable the distribution of responsibility for leadership and develop teachers as leaders can also influence the distribution of leadership. In the elementary schools in the Distributed Leadership Study, school leaders formed new leadership positions or rewrote the job description for existing positions in order to distribute responsibility for leadership functions and routines in their schools. Realizing that they could not take on every leadership routine, school leaders enlisted the support of others by creating new full-time leadership positions or redesigning existing positions. At Adams School, for example, Brenda Williams arranged for other leaders to take on responsibility for disciplining students and ensuring that students came to school in a timely manner. This was important so that

Williams could focus on leadership activities that were directly tied to improving the quality of classroom instruction. Student discipline and student attendance were important to Williams, but she could not address them adequately and still commit significant time and energy to improving instruction.

The distribution of responsibility for leadership does not always involve the creation of a new administrative or specialist position. School leaders also formed new leadership roles that were filled by teachers who either had full-time teaching duties or had released time from teaching to perform their leadership responsibilities. At schools in the Distributed Leadership Study, these roles included grade-level leader, literacy or reading lead teacher, mathematics lead teacher, local school council representative, after-school program coordinator, and other subject-specific teacher leaders. Some teachers who took on these roles had released time from teaching. Other teachers taught full-time while they juggled their leadership responsibilities. Some received stipends, while others received no additional compensation.

The manner in which teachers found their way into these leadership roles also differed, depending on the position and the school. In some schools, teachers voted their peers into leadership positions, while in others, leadership appointments were based entirely on who volunteered. For some positions, such as lead literacy or mathematics teacher or grade-level leader, some combination of senior administrators' selection, volunteerism, and staff election was usually in play, though it varied by school. Some positions were highly coveted, while others were less desirable, requiring methods beyond taking volunteers to fill the full slate of leadership roles. There was some evidence of school leaders hiring teachers with a view toward cultivating teacher leadership. At Adams School, for example, the recruitment of a new upper-grade science teacher focused not only on science teaching ability but also on the person's ability to provide leadership for science education at the school.

The creation of structures and routines that enable teachers to take on leadership responsibilities and thus hone teachers' leadership skills can also contribute to the distribution of responsibility for leadership functions and routines. Heller and Firestone (1995) found that teacher leadership developed in some of the schools in their study through the creation of committees staffed by teachers that were designed to support the implementation of a reform. Similarly, in some schools in the Distributed Leadership Study, leaders in some schools designed and implemented a variety of structures that enabled teachers to take responsibility for some key leadership functions. At Adams School, for example, Williams and her leadership team invented the Breakfast Club to provide professional development for teachers. The Breakfast Club was designed so that a classroom teacher always took responsibility for facilitating the discussion among staff. The Breakfast Club provided a regular opportunity for teachers to lead and a place for teachers to develop their leadership skills. Committed to "developing indigenous faculty leadership," Principal Lance Stern at Baxter Elementary School created an elaborate infrastructure to engage teachers in leading instructional improvement at the school. This infrastructure included a faculty leadership group to which each grade level elected a teacher; bimonthly grade-level meetings; a literacy subcommittee; and a mathematics and science subcommittee. Teachers played an active role in each of these venues. While the faculty leadership group focused on whole-school initiatives, such as school improvement planning, budgeting, and building professional community, the subcommittees worked on leading improvements in particular school subjects. In Stern's view, teacher leadership was a critical component in developing leadership for instruction, but teacher leadership would not happen without an infrastructure that enabled it, so he worked to build that infrastructure.

While there is evidence that formal structure can contribute to the distribution of responsibility for leadership by enabling teachers to take on leadership responsibilities, it may not be a necessary condition. Transforming the culture of a school can also be an important enabling condition for teacher leadership (Heller and Firestone, 1995). The creation of professional norms in schools that enable and support teachers in taking on leadership responsibilities is thought to contribute to the distribution of leadership among formal leaders and teachers (Harris and Lambert, 2003; Hargreaves, 1991; Little, 1990; Rosenholtz, 1989).

Research suggests that parents (Rogoff, Turkanis, and Bartlett, 2001), other external agents such as comprehensive school reform models (Camburn, Rowan, and Taylor, 2003), and the policy environment (Portin, Schneider, DeArmond, and Gundlach, 2003) can also enable (and, of course, constrain) the distribution of leadership in schools. For example, Camburn, Rowan, and Taylor (2003) suggest that schools that implement a comprehensive school reform model configure formal leadership positions differently than non-CSR schools. Furthermore, participation in a CSR model involves a higher level of leadership for instruction, much of which is tied to the creation of CSR-specific positions. However, there are also differences among the CSR models in that the America's Choice and Success for All models created more leadership positions than the Accelerated Schools Program or comparison schools in the study. America's Choice and Success for All schools had approximately four leaders, while comparison schools and Accelerated Schools Program schools had 2.5 leaders on average.

Distribution of Leadership by Default

Leadership is not always distributed according to the grand designs of principals, head teachers, or other administrators. Likewise, planning and design are not always essential for the distribution of leadership among formal leaders and teachers. At times, savvy administrators, specialists, or classroom teachers, acting alone or collectively, may identify an area in which leadership is lacking and step in to fill the vacuum. This direction may result because these individuals see a particular leadership function or routine falling through the cracks or because they believe that beefing up some aspect of leadership is critical to the school's success.

Based on a study of reform in Canadian and U.S. schools, Hargreaves and Fink (2004) found that sometimes teachers fill in leadership gaps that occur when their principal lacks the requisite skills in a particular area. At Baxter Elementary (a school in the Distributed Leadership Study), an assistant principal, Pat Brandon, recognized that principal Lance Stern was not a "people person." Despite Stern's elaborate infrastructure, which gave teachers a voice and a role in efforts to improve instruction at Baxter, teachers regularly spoke about his poor communication skills. Hearing this from teachers and seeing it in her daily work at the school, Brandon took it upon herself to be the communicator and people person, establishing a good rapport with teachers and taking time to talk with them about school policies and programs. In this way, Brandon took on leadership responsibilities, unknown to the principal and certainly not at his bidding. Thus, positional leaders, teachers, or indeed others such as parents or school boards can take responsibility for leadership functions or routines that are not being fulfilled by others.

Of course, explicit defaulting on particular leadership functions is not always necessary for such arrangements to evolve. As people get to know one another, they figure out working relationships, and new responsibilities for leadership functions and routines emerge with time. Individuals who work together learn to trust one another and appreciate one another's strengths and weaknesses. As a result, "intuitive working relations" develop that contribute to the distribution of leadership among individuals (Gronn, 2003, p. 4).

Distribution of Leadership Through Crisis

Sometimes unanticipated events that pose a crisis for a school or that simply must be addressed contribute to the distribution of leadership among people. A school's achievement scores in reading decline dramatically. Administrators discover drugs in the school. Teachers apprehend a student with a firearm. Events like these demand immediate attention. School administrators react immediately to avert a crisis. They may create an ad hoc committee of teachers and school administrators to address the issue, bringing together individuals who do not typically work together to address a particular leadership function. This can change the distribution of leadership among administrators and teachers in the school.

Gronn (2003) calls the distribution resulting from situations like this *spontaneous collaboration*. It is impromptu. It is often transient, because these types of collaboration are motivated by particular challenges; once the challenge is addressed, the group disbands.

What Makes a Leader Influential?

We know a considerable amount about why teachers construct others, both formally designated leaders and other teachers, as influential leaders. If responsibility for the performance of leadership work is distributed among individuals, some with formal positions and others without such positions, how do some individuals get constructed as influential leaders by teachers? Teachers do not always identify the individuals who help in the performance of leadership routines or who have formal responsibility for particular leadership functions as influential leaders when it comes to their classroom work. Similarly, some who perform leadership routines and are deemed influential by teachers do not hold formally designated leadership positions. Of the eighty-four teachers studied in the first year of the Distributed Leadership Study, seventy (83.3 percent) identified the principal as an influential leader for their teaching practice, while twenty-four (28.6 percent) mentioned the assistant principal as an influential leader. At the same time, sixty-seven teachers (79.8 percent) identified other teachers as influential leaders for their teaching (Spillane, Hallett, and Diamond,

2003). While formal position was a factor in teachers constructing school administrators as influential leaders for their own instruction, it was not a sufficient condition: only seven of eighty-four teachers in the first year of the study (8.3 percent) cited position alone when constructing administrators as influential leaders for their teaching (Spillane, Hallett, and Diamond, 2003).

Especially helpful in figuring out how leadership is constructed is investigating leadership from the perspective of followers and trying to tease out what makes some individuals influential leaders. Teachers construct others as influential leaders based on their interactions with them as well as conversations with colleagues about these individuals. Teachers base their constructions on forms of human, cultural, social, and economic capital (Spillane, Hallett, and Diamond, 2003).

- *Human capital* involves a person's knowledge, skills, and expertise.

- *Cultural capital* refers to a person's way of being and doing, interactive styles that are valued in particular contexts.

- *Social capital* refers to a person's social networks or connections but also concerns the prevalence of norms such as trust, collaboration, and a sense of obligation among individuals in an organization.

- *Economic capital* includes money and other material resources, including books, curricular materials, and computers, among other things.

Teachers' perception of principals' expertise or human capital is one factor in the extent to which teachers see principals as an influence on their teaching. Principals' interactive styles or cultural capital can motivate teacher change (Johnson and Venable, 1986; Treslan and Ryan, 1986). Blase and his colleagues found that principals who engage in practices such as soliciting advice and opinions while also praising teachers better motivate teachers to improve instruction (Blase and Blase, 1998; Blase and Kirby, 1992).

Research also identifies social capital as a basis of teachers' influence as leaders (Little, 1982; Rosenholtz, 1989; Johnson, 1990; Louis, Marks, and Kruse, 1996). Specifically, social capital in the form of valued social networks, mutual trust and respect, and a sense of obligation and responsibility is especially important when it comes to teacher leadership for instruction (Smylie and Hart, 1999).

While teachers in the Distributed Leadership Study constructed school administrators as leaders based largely on cultural capital, the teachers in the study constructed other teachers as leaders based on a mix of human, social, and cultural capital. Of the eighty-four teachers we interviewed, fifty-nine (70.2 percent) mentioned cultural capital when constructing the principal or assistant principal as influential, whereas eighteen (21.4 percent) cited human capital, thirteen (15.5 percent) cited social capital, and twenty (23.8 percent) cited economic capital. A teacher pointed to the importance of cultural capital in identifying her principal as an influential leader when she remarked, "It's just the way you say it and do it, I guess . . . the way they come across and talk to you; I guess I'm just a fool for people knowing how to talk to you and to give you that kind of respect and you get these things done." Cultural capital—valued interactive style—was especially important in teachers' construction of other teachers and administrators as influential leaders.

Thirty-eight of the eighty-four teachers we interviewed (just over 45 percent) cited human capital in constructing other teachers as influential leaders, whereas fifty (59.5 percent) identified cultural capital, forty-two (50 percent) cited social capital, and twenty-three (27.4 percent) mentioned economic capital. One teacher highlighted the importance of human capital for teacher leaders in her comments: "Mrs. Rodriguez is very knowledgeable in science. And she has a lot of ideas about science. Mrs. Diaz is a strong language arts person. So, you know, whenever I have a question or . . . want to know about how to go about a strategy a particular way, I might ask her, 'Well, how do you do this?'"

Conclusion

The empirical knowledge base on distributed leadership is still relatively small, although it has grown considerably in recent years. Much of the work has been conducted in elementary or primary schools. Most of it has centered on the leader-plus aspect of a distributed perspective.

This work has generated important insights into how responsibility for leadership work is distributed in schools. Three to seven formally designated leaders typically take responsibility for leadership routines. Informal leaders, usually classroom teachers, also take responsibility for leadership routines. The distribution of leadership among formally designated leaders and informal leaders differs according to the leadership routine, the school subject, the type of school, the school's size, and the school or school leadership team's developmental stage. The distribution of responsibility for leadership routines come to pass in at least three ways—strict division of labor, co-performance, and parallel performance. The distribution of responsibility for leadership can happen by design, by default, and through crisis. Finally, teachers construct others, both formally designated leaders and individuals with no formal leadership designation, as influential leaders based on valued forms of human, cultural, social, and economic capital. All of these insights are best thought of as hypotheses that merit further investigation and testing.

However, adopting the leader-plus framework by itself is insufficient. A distributed perspective presses us to look not only at who takes responsibility for particular leadership routines and functions but also how the *practice* of leadership takes form in the interactions of these leaders with followers and with the situation. I will address this issue in detail in Chapter Three.

Note

1. *Comprehensive school reform*, or *whole school reform*, refers to externally developed reform models that are adopted by schools in an effort to improve student achievement—for example, Success for All, America's Choice, and the Accelerated Schools Program.

3

The Practice Aspect

Setting the Scene

On a bright November afternoon, the literacy committee is convening in the school library at Adams School, as they do every five weeks or so. Approximately twenty teachers, representing each of the K–8 grade levels, are present, along with the designated leaders for the meeting: the principal, the literacy coordinator, the African American heritage coordinator, and a third-grade teacher who is seen by both administrators and teachers as an influential leader for literacy instruction. Established to engage teachers in decision-making activities in regard to literacy instruction, the literacy committee has meetings that are typically co-facilitated by some combination of the literacy coordinator, the principal, the African American heritage coordinator, and one or more of the assistant principals.

Brenda Williams, the principal, gets things rolling in a good-humored but businesslike manner, previewing the agenda for the afternoon's meeting. With reference to one of the agenda items, Williams notes that there will be time for teachers to share stories of their attempts to put "strategies that work" into practice. "We've found that the things we have learned best we learn through sharing," Williams remarks, echoing a familiar refrain in her work at Adams School.

Next up is the literacy coordinator, who congratulates teachers, noting that all grade levels have shown improvement in the most recent five-week assessment in literacy. She goes on to identify areas of strength and weakness in student results by grade level, encouraging teachers to attend to areas in which students appear to be having difficulty and identifying specific resources that teachers can use in this work. Williams listens to and endorses the literacy coordinator's message with frequent affirming nods.

The African American heritage coordinator takes over next, reviewing, at the request of the literacy coordinator, Chapter Six of *Strategies That Work: Teaching Comprehension to Enhance Understanding* by Stephanie Harvey and Anne Goudvis. The teachers are to have read the chapter for today's meeting, which focuses on the importance of helping students make connections in literacy instruction. The African American heritage coordinator draws examples from her own reading with her niece to illustrate the three sorts of connections that teachers should help students make when reading texts. Teachers energetically offer suggestions and examples from their classrooms. One teacher argues that it is important that teachers be explicit with students about the strategy they are teaching so that students understand what it means to make connections. Williams interjects, noting that while the "making connections" strategy is important, it is imperative that teachers "don't just jump to the strategy" in their classrooms. She reminds teachers of the sequence: "teacher models, guided practice, scaffolding, and then independent application of strategy." Another teacher offers an example from her teaching of how the making connections strategy might play out in practice. Other teachers chime in with vivid examples from their own classrooms, and leaders offer their perspective on these accounts from the classroom.

Later in the meeting, the teacher leader moves center stage and, with laminated posters, makes a presentation on using graphic organizers in the classroom. At the request of the literacy coordinator, who is constantly picking up teaching strategies at conferences and meetings, this teacher leader has begun to teach graphic organizers in her classroom. Acknowledging the difficulties with using the new tool, she proceeds to describe an activity she has used successfully in her classroom to overcome some of the difficulties. It is clear from her materials and presentation that she has spent considerable time piecing together today's talk. At various points during this presentation, Williams and the literacy coordinator interrupt to draw teachers' attention to the importance of familiarizing students with graphic organizers in order to help students' performance on the Illinois Standards Achievement Test (ISAT) and how particular skills connect with standards and the school's teaching framework. Toward the end of this stage of the meeting, at the invitation of the literacy coordinator, teachers decide, through voting, that making connections should be the focus of the next five-week assessment and that they should engage in small-group work to prepare for this.[1]

Shifting Focus to Leadership Practice

Some readers might not recognize instances of leadership in the opening scenario; it lacks heroines performing gallant acts to move the school toward new horizons. Instead, the four leaders at Adams are engaged in the rather mundane work of identifying and promoting approaches to teaching literacy that may contribute to improvements in student achievement. For me, as outlined in my definition of leadership in Chapter One, this *is* leadership, and more specifically, it is leadership practice. It is leadership because the leaders involved intend to influence teachers' literacy teaching in order to transform students' opportunities to learn to read and write at Adams; teachers understand it as an attempt to influence their teaching; and it is tied to the core work of the school—instruction. The opening scenario displays leadership practice in that practice is exemplified in the interactions among participants.

The opening scenario captures how multiple leaders co-perform the routine of the literacy committee meeting. As defined in Chapter One, a routine refers to a repeated and recognizable pattern of interdependent actions that involves two or more people. We found evidence of co-performance of leadership routines in all schools in the Distributed Leadership Study. We might characterize the co-performance in the opening scenario by identifying and labeling the different actions and roles evident in what Williams, the literacy coordinator, the African American heritage coordinator, and the lead teacher are doing. Based on this and other instances of leadership practice at Adams School, we would observe that Williams's roles include setting instructional expectations for teachers and keeping literacy standards front and center, while the literacy coordinator, who also performs these roles, brings new teaching strategies and resources to the attention of teachers. This type of analysis would enable us to identify role differentiation and role overlap among these four leaders in co-performing leadership routines related to literacy. However, counting in and counting up the actions or roles of these four leaders is unsatisfactory in analyzing practice from a distributed perspective. Interactions are key; therefore, it is essential to analyze leadership practice from the level of the group or collective. It is only when we analyze the collective leadership practice that we can see how the practice takes shape in the interactions as distinct from the actions of individuals. Additive models fail to notice and investigate these interactions.

What is striking in the opening scenario is the manner in which the practice takes form in the interactions among the four leaders. While the actions of these four leaders are important, it is in the interactions among them that leadership practice gets constructed. The leaders in the opening scenario build on one another's contributions, collectively constituting leadership practice in their improvised responses to one another. In this way, leadership practice is stretched over these leaders rather than simply being a function of their individual actions.

Regrettably, the empirical knowledge base on the practice aspect of distributed leadership is thin. Few have investigated how leadership takes shape in the interactions among leaders, followers, and their situation; most of the work in this area has been done by me and by Gronn and his colleagues (Gronn, 2002, 2003; Spillane, Diamond, and Jita, 2000, 2003; Spillane, Diamond, Sherer, and Coldren, 2004; Goldstein, 2004). This chapter attempts to redress this absence by looking first at the people dimension, then at the situation dimension of interactions in leadership practice.

The People Dimension

People, whether in leader or in follower roles, are central to any analysis of leadership practice. What people do—the actions they take—are critical. But all too often, attempts to analyze leadership practice never go beyond the actions of individuals—usually, individual leaders—or some attempt to aggregate the actions of two or more leaders. In a distributed approach, it is also critical to look at how leadership practice takes shape in the interactions between leaders and followers.

Understanding Interactions: Unpacking the "In Between"

From a distributed perspective, exploring leadership practice is not a simple task. A critical challenge involves unpacking how leadership practice is stretched over leaders. One way to do this is by analyzing the interdependencies among leaders' actions (Gronn, 2002, 2003; Spillane, Diamond, and Jita, 2000, 2003). Researchers have examined the interdependencies between activities and the interdependencies that arise from resources that are tied to multiple activities (Lawrence and Lorsch, 1986; Malone and Crowston, 1994; Malone and others, 1999; March and Simon, 1958; Thompson,

1967).[2] Thompson (1967) identifies three types of interdependencies between activities:

- *Reciprocal interdependencies*, in which each activity requires inputs from the other

- *Pooled interdependencies*, in which activities share or produce common resources but are otherwise independent

- *Sequential interdependencies*, in which some activities depend on the completion of others[3]

Analyzing interdependencies, however, only gets us so far in understanding how the collective operates in leadership practice. The human dimension of interactions falls through the cracks when the actions of people are brought to the fore, and how interactions come about goes unexplored. The challenge is to capture how leaders work as a group. It is critical to analyze leadership practice at the collective level. The group of leaders in the opening scenario has properties that enable and constrain their co-performance of the routine; hence, it is essential to move beyond an analysis of individual actions and knowledge and consider the collective. If an important unit of analysis for examining leadership practice is leaders in particular situations working with followers and artifacts—the collective, rather than individual leaders abstracted from their situations—then getting from an analysis of interdependencies to the workings of the group of leaders involves a stretch of the imagination, to say the least.

In analyzing interactions among leaders in the co-performance of leadership practice, it is necessary to attend to both the workings of the collective and its component parts. With respect to the opening scenario, we need to understand how the principal, the literacy coordinator, the African American heritage coordinator, and the teacher leader function as a collective. How do these four leaders manage to work together, attending to one another's actions?

How do they co-perform the leadership routine? The notion of *heed-fulness* is especially helpful in this regard (Weick and Roberts, 1993).[4] Heedfulness describes the way in which a set of behaviors is performed: groups act heedfully when they act carefully, intelligently, purposefully, and attentively. Weick and Roberts (1993) argue that individuals who act like a group "interrelate their actions with more or less care" and in this interrelating, we can begin to identify how the group functions as a collective (p. 360).

Members of a group have a sense of themselves as an ensemble or collective. They don't just think about their individual actions but think about what they do in terms of other members of the group. Weick and Roberts identify three interrelated processes involved in groups acting more or less heedfully:

- Group members create the social norms between group members by acting as though these norms exist.

- Acting as though there are social norms, people construct their actions by envisioning a system of joint action and connect that constructed action with the system they envisioned.

- The result is a system of practice that resides not just in the individuals but also in the interrelating or interacting between their actions.

In this way, the co-performance of leadership is stretched over leaders. I prefer the term *co-performance* to the term *joint action* because *joint action* implies shared goals, whereas *co-performance* allows for the possibility that those performing the routine might, intentionally or unintentionally, pursue different or even contrary goals.

The more heedful interrelating or interactions take place in a group, the more capable the group is of intelligent practice (Weick and Roberts, 1993). With respect to the interactions among leaders in the literacy committee meeting, for example, we might argue that the participants construct a mutually shared field. Within this field, members of the group improvise, playing off one another's actions.

Analyzing interactions among leaders in the co-performance of leadership practice, my colleagues and I (Spillane, Diamond, and Jita, 2000, 2003; Spillane, Diamond, Sherer, and Coldren, 2004) have identified three types of distribution:

- *Collaborated distribution* characterizes leadership practice that is stretched over the work of two or more leaders who work together in place and time to execute the same leadership routine, such as facilitating a faculty meeting. The co-practice in this situation is similar to that in basketball, in which players must interact with one another, passing to teammates when they stop dribbling and working to set one another up to shoot.

- *Collective distribution* characterizes practice that is stretched over the work of two or more leaders who enact a leadership routine by working separately but interdependently. The interdependencies are akin to those in baseball or cricket, in which players at bat perform alone, but their actions in interaction with that of the pitcher or bowler collectively produce the practice.

- *Coordinated distribution* refers to leadership routines that involve activities that have to be performed in a particular sequence. The interdependency in this situation is similar to that in a relay race in track; the co-performance of the relay race depends on a particular ordered sequence.

These three types of distribution are not mutually exclusive; a single leadership routine could involve more than one type.[5]

Each type of distribution—collaborated, collective, and coordinated—involves different sorts of interdependencies that pose both similar and different challenges for leadership practice. Research on groups suggests that practices involving collaborated distribution may require much more attention to the affective dimension. Situations involving collaborated distribution require leaders to co-perform in public, accentuating the affective dimension of interactions among leaders, whereas situations involving collective distribution allow leaders to co-perform separately, potentially downplaying the affective dynamic.

These distributions also pose different challenges with respect to the heedfulness of the interrelating among participants. In situations of collaborated distribution, for example, leaders co-performing a leadership routine have multiple opportunities to assess their colleagues' perspectives and actions firsthand. These circumstances can increase the opportunities for more heedful interrelating among leaders. In contrast, situations involving collective distribution, in which leaders have fewer opportunities to observe one another in action, offer fewer opportunities to increase the heedfulness of the interacting. Indeed, the likelihood of heedless interacting is perhaps greater in situations involving collective distribution compared with those involving collaborated distribution. The heedfulness of the interacting among leaders in collective distribution situations depends on the accuracy of leaders' reports to one another about what they do separately but interdependently.

Collaborated Distribution

In collaborated distribution, the leadership practice involves leaders co-performing a leadership routine together in the same time and place. Collaborated distribution involves a reciprocal interdependency, in which the actions of different leaders involve input from one another in co-performing a leadership routine. Reciprocal interdependencies involve individuals playing off one another in the same place and time, with the action of person A directly and immediately enabling (or potentially constraining) the action of person B and vice versa. It resembles the interdependencies between partners in the two-step dance discussed in Chapter One, although considering the number of people involved in the performance, square dancing may be a better analogy.

Collaborated practice is evident in many of the leadership routines for literacy at Adams School, such as the literacy committee meeting in the opening scenario. While the roles and actions of the four leaders converge and diverge at different points in the meeting, it is in the interactions among leaders that the practice takes shape. Recall the teacher leader's presentation on teaching graphic organizers in the classroom. At one point during this section of the meeting, the literacy coordinator interrupts. Building on the teacher leader's presentation, the literacy coordinator draws teachers' attention to the importance of students' knowing how to use graphic organizers in order to perform well on state assessments. The literacy coordinator's action supplements and extends the teacher leader's action. This is evidence of heedful interrelating in that the literacy coordinator's actions appear to be mindful of and attentive to the teacher leader's actions. The same holds for the principal's actions during this portion of the meeting. As I will argue later in this chapter, leaders can be heedful of one another's actions without necessarily agreeing or responding in a way that is supportive of those actions. In my usage, unlike Weick and Roberts's usage, *heedfulness* or *mindfulness* does not imply agreement or supportiveness but merely implies attentiveness and responsiveness to another's actions.

To underscore the importance of the interactions among the leaders' actions, consider the focus of the leadership practice in the discussion of graphic organizers. The leadership practice in this instance focuses simultaneously on motivating teachers and developing their capacity to teach graphic organizers. Through their heedful interacting, the lead teacher, the literacy coordinator, and Williams are able to simultaneously focus on teacher motivation and capacity to teach graphic organizers. If we focus only on the actions of each leader, we notice that both teacher motivation and capacity are addressed in this leadership practice. However, focusing only on leaders' actions would ignore how motivation and capacity are woven together in the leadership practice, because this is accomplished in the interactions among the leaders.

We might take an additional step and explore efforts to build teacher capacity in the literacy committee routine. Specifically, we can analyze the knowledge that leaders are trying to develop in this instance of leadership practice. Williams's actions and some of the actions of the literacy coordinator focus on what Lee Shulman (1986, 1987) terms *curricular knowledge*—for example, knowledge of student assessment and knowledge of standards. *Curricular knowledge* refers to things such as programs designed for the teaching of particular subjects and topics at a given level, the instructional materials available, and the characteristics that serve as indications for the use of particular curriculum or program materials in particular circumstances. The African American heritage coordinator's actions and some of the literacy coordinator's actions focus on pedagogical knowledge in regard to literacy, with a slant toward *outsider knowledge* (knowledge from research and external experts). The teacher leader's actions also focused on pedagogical knowledge, but with a slant toward *insider knowledge* (knowledge generated from classroom practice) (Cochran-Smith and Lytle, 1993). The problem with conducting the analysis in this way, however, is that it fails to capture the manner in which these different types of knowledge are intertwined in the leadership practice observed in this instance of the literacy committee meeting. Attending to the interactions among leaders, however, it becomes clear that the curricular knowledge is grounded in the discussion of the pedagogical knowledge and that this was accomplished through the heedful interacting of the four leaders, whose actions supplemented, assisted, and gave meaning to one another. Hence, it seems reasonable to argue that the practice of leadership was stretched over the teacher leader, the principal, the African American heritage coordinator, and the literacy coordinator rather than enacted by each of them separately.

We found evidence of collaborated distribution at all of our research sites, although the type of distribution depended on the leadership routine. In some routines, such as teacher development and curriculum committee meetings, collaborated distribution was more common than in other leadership routines, such as monitoring or evaluating instruction.

Collective Distribution

In collective distribution, the leadership practice involves leaders who work separately but interdependently to co-perform a leadership routine. While all leadership routines might be said to involve collective practice, I reserve the term for situations in which two or more leaders are co-performing a routine but not in the same place or at the same time. Interdependence is not confined to here-and-now interactions.

Collective distribution was evident in all schools in the Distributed Leadership Study, although it again depended on the particular leadership routine. The performance of routines such as instructional monitoring and evaluation, teacher development, and identification and establishment of instructional priorities often involved collective distribution.

The teacher evaluation routine at Ellis School, alluded to in Chapter One, is an example of collective distribution. The principal and assistant principal agree that evaluating teaching is critical in forging instructional improvement at Ellis School. Working separately but interdependently and heedful of each other's actions, these two leaders co-perform the teacher evaluation routine.

The principal believes that two annual visits to a classroom—the school district's legal requirement—are inadequate to evaluate a teacher's practice. Further, she is convinced that the required annual evaluation perpetuates the "dog and pony show" syndrome—that is, teachers' putting on two showcase lessons annually. As a result, the lessons the principal observes during her twice-a-year evaluation excursions to Ellis classrooms do not capture the realities of instruction. In an effort to ameliorate this situation and tie the teacher evaluation routine more directly to the teacher development function, the principal and assistant principal work together on evaluating teachers. They co-perform the teacher evaluation routine and, in the process, have fundamentally transformed the practice of evaluating teachers' instruction at Ellis.

The assistant principal has a friendly and informal rapport with teachers. He visits classrooms regularly. He "makes the rounds" two or three times a day, often sitting in on lessons and providing feedback to teachers. He explains:

> I'm more involved in the formative evaluation of teachers, where I will observe teachers, talk to them prior to an observation. Observe teachers, and then they might tell me certain things to look for, that they need help in this area or that area. And then we'll meet after. . . . So I try to visit every classroom every day. . . . I do my best, you know, to be visible, 'cause you can pick up a lot just by those informal type observations of just seeing what's going on. . . . So, you know, that helps improve instruction.

What the assistant principal does might be best described as formative evaluation. On the other hand, the principal works on summative evaluation, visiting classrooms twice per year to evaluate the quality of teachers' instructional practices. Teachers at Ellis revere the principal, referring to her as "doctor." When she enters a meeting, chatter ceases, and she gets the undivided attention of her staff.

Seeing these summative and formative evaluation activities as independent would misrepresent and distort the practice of evaluating teachers at Ellis School. Specifically, the practice of evaluating instruction at Ellis School must be understood in the interactions between the principal's actions in conducting summative evaluations and the assistant principal's actions in conducting formative evaluations. The assistant principal and principal pool the insights and knowledge gleaned from their classroom visits through formal and informal meetings. Combining their knowledge, they develop an understanding of each teacher's classroom practice and develop an appreciation for the development needs of their staff. As the assistant principal put it, "Through a formative process and a summative process, we take a look at all of our teachers."

Working separately, these two leaders co-perform the teacher evaluation routine at Ellis School. Attentive to how their individual actions fit within a larger system of practice for evaluating teachers, these two leaders act interdependently, heedful of how each other's actions ultimately fit into their collective practice. In this way, the practice of teacher evaluation is stretched over their separate but interdependent actions. Thus, while the two may go for an extended time without directly interacting in regard to teacher evaluation, their actions are linked because the design and execution of one dimension is intimately related to the design and execution of the other. Teacher evaluation at Ellis School involves a pooled interdependency, in which separate but interdependent practices are essential in the co-performance of the teacher evaluation routine.

Coordinated Distribution

In coordinated distribution, the leadership practice involves leaders co-performing a leadership routine in which they work separately or together on sequentially arranged leadership tasks that are necessary for the performance of the routine. The completion of multiple interdependent activities arranged sequentially is critical in co-performing many leadership routines.

The Five-Week Assessment leadership routine at Adams School illustrates how leadership practice can be stretched over leadership activities across time. The Five-Week Assessment routine involves seven steps that are performed in a particular order:

- The literacy coordinator creates the student assessment instrument for reading and writing.

- Teachers administer the assessment instrument to students.

- The literacy coordinator and her assistant score and analyze the results.

- The principal and literacy coordinator meet to discuss the assessment results; using information from their observations of classroom instruction, they interpret and make sense of the data and diagnose problems with the literacy program.

- The literacy coordinator compiles resources and strategies that might enable teachers to address some of the problems identified through the analysis of the assessment data and classroom observation data.

- Working with a lead teacher and the African American heritage coordinator, the literacy coordinator reports assessment results to teachers during literacy committee meetings.

- The literacy coordinator, principal, and teachers interpret assessment results and identify and agree to instructional strategies that might address the problems they have identified.

The Five-Week Assessment routine involves a number of interdependent, sequenced components, illustrating how leadership practice can be stretched temporally over sequenced and coordinated activities. Each of these activities depends on resources generated from a prior activity. Multiple interdependent tasks, arranged sequentially, are critical to the performance of the leadership routine.

Pulling Together or in Different Directions?

The preceding examples focus on co-performance of leadership routines in which leaders were pulling together, in similar directions. However, leaders can and do pull in opposite or different directions.[6] Leaders can strive for different or even conflicting ends while working in parallel or even while co-performing leadership routines. Most of us know of situations in which one group of leaders in a school promote one instructional vision, while another group of leaders work in parallel at selling another, sometimes conflicting vision. In addition, leaders can co-perform a leadership routine in the same place and time but still promote different ends—for example, different visions. At times, conflicts are aired in public, but at other times, they remain under the table, evident only to savvy insiders.

Recall the situation at Kosten School, in which a new principal and new assistant principal initiated new routines that were designed to transform instruction—for example, monitoring instruction and reviewing teachers' lesson plans. Some teachers resisted these efforts and engaged in leadership practice that was designed to preserve the status quo in the face of attempts to transform it. Some might see these situations as the antithesis of a distributed perspective on leadership. I don't share this view. A distributed perspective applies to leadership at Kosten School as easily as it does to leadership practice at Adams School, where, at the time of our study, formally designated leaders and informal leaders were roughly on the same page with respect to school vision and instructional improvement. A distributed perspective on leadership does not privilege situations in which leaders are pulling together over situations in which they are pulling in different or even opposing directions.

Compared with situations involving collaborated distribution, situations involving collective or coordinated distribution may lend themselves more easily to leaders co-performing leadership routines while striving for different ends. One can imagine how the teacher evaluation at Ellis School might have turned out differently if the assistant principal and principal had been promoting two very different kinds of instruction. The fact that the leaders work separately in place and time to perform a routine such as teacher evaluation can allow this to happen. However, the evidence from Kosten School suggests that even in situations of collaborated distribution, leaders can pull in opposing directions.

Seeking different ends, the two leadership camps at Kosten still co-performed some leadership routines, such as faculty meetings, and at times clashed publicly. Focusing on the formally designated leaders, we might argue that the principal and assistant principal are the leaders co-performing the leadership routines in these situations and that the two teachers who are working to preserve the status quo are not co-performing the leadership routine. But concentrating exclusively on formally designated leaders and on the designed as distinct from the lived organization is problematic. Teachers at Kosten recognize leadership not only in the change efforts of the principal and assistant principal but also in the preservation efforts of informal teacher leaders. At one level, because the groups are seeking different ends, we might argue that leadership practice is stretched over leaders in camp A (principal and assistant principal) and stretched over leaders in camp B (teachers working to preserve the status quo), analyzing the co-performance within each group. But leaders don't have to see eye to eye to co-perform a leadership routine. Hence, at another level, we can argue that the practice was stretched over leaders in both camps, even though they were striving for different ends.

Although leaders at Kosten were pulling in opposing directions, the leaders, regardless of the ends they sought, were still heedful of one another's actions. Although they did not share the same goals (in fact, they sought opposing goals), they shared the experience. The teachers working to preserve the status quo played off the actions of the principal and assistant principal while working for different ends. Being heedful of another leader's practice does not necessarily entail responding in a way that is supportive of that practice. As I argued earlier, situations of collaborated distribution involve a reciprocal interdependency, with different leaders playing off one another's actions. Although they sought conflicting ends, the informal teacher leaders at Kosten played off the actions of the principal and assistant principal, and vice versa, in the co-performance of some leadership routines. Whether they sought similar or different ends, the actions of one leader enabled or constrained the actions of another. In this way, leadership practice is stretched over leaders who seek different and even conflicting ends. Understanding how leadership practice is stretched over leaders is as critical in these sorts of situations as it is in situations in which leaders are pulling together.

Leaders don't have to see eye to eye to be on the same page or even have to get along with one another to co-perform leadership routines such as selling an instructional vision or developing teachers' knowledge of mathematics or science education. Leadership practice is stretched over leaders even when they are not striving for the same ends. When leaders don't see eye to eye, they still function as a collective in the co-performance of leadership routines. From a distributed perspective, the challenge is to understand how practice takes shape in the interactions of a group of leaders, recognizing that whether they seek similar, different, or even conflicting goals is only one dimension of any such analysis.

Followers

Up to now, I have concerned myself chiefly with school leaders. Reflecting the state of the literature, my attention to followers is limited. My own work to date has focused chiefly on conceptualizing how leaders co-perform leadership routines, and only recently have I started to work on analyzing the role of followers in leadership practice. In this section, I briefly address followers and how they contribute to defining leadership practice in their interactions with leaders.

Some scholars find the leader-follower distinction problematic because social influence is a two-way street. While such worries are warranted, my fear is that if the distinction is ignored altogether, the role of followers in defining leadership practice will fall through the cracks. My own data suggest that teachers, specialists, and administrators do construct others as leaders (whether formal or informal), depending on the particular circumstance, so the distinction between leaders and followers appears to be real enough in schools.

Attention to followers is also important in our investigation of interactions in leadership practice. In the literacy committee meeting at Adams School, classroom teachers were active participants, interacting frequently with the four leaders by offering examples and suggestions. During the review of strategies for helping students to make connections, for example, a teacher responded to the African American heritage coordinator's presentation by noting that it is important to be explicit with students about the strategy one is teaching. Acknowledging the importance of what the teacher had said, Williams went on to remind teachers not to jump to presenting a strategy but to follow the school's instructional sequence: modeling, guided practice, scaffolding, and application. Williams's statement makes sense only in the context of the teacher's remarks. At this point, another teacher gave an example of how this sequence might play out when using the making connections strategy in the classroom. What we see here is leaders and followers supplementing and extending one another's actions through heedful interrelating. Hence, leaders collectively constitute their practice in interaction with followers, and in this way, followers contribute to defining leadership practice.

Looking at multiple literacy committee meetings (and some other leadership routines related to literacy) at Adams over a five-year period, patterns are evident in the nature of interactions among leaders and followers. The opening scenario is representative of the interrelating among the literacy coordinator, the principal, the

African American heritage coordinator, and the teacher leader, as well as the interactions among leaders and classroom teachers. As these individuals play off one another, there is a reciprocal relationship among their actions, and it is through this interrelating that the leadership practice takes shape.

Curricular Domains Matter in Interactions

The nature of the interactions among leaders and among leaders and followers differs, depending on the subject area (Spillane, 2005). Recall the literacy committee meeting at Adams School. In this leadership routine, there is a lively, back-and-forth dialogue among participants, including administrators, specialists, teacher leaders, and teachers. This is characteristic of literacy-related leadership routines in general at the school. While leaders' actions are at times similar, there are also differences in their actions; some leaders focus mostly on developing teachers' pedagogical knowledge, while others work on motivating teachers and developing their curricular knowledge. Taken together, leaders' interactions center on motivating teachers to teach particular content, setting expectations for literacy instruction, identifying instructional resources, and developing teachers' curricular and pedagogical knowledge. Classroom teachers are regular contributors to literacy meetings. They use examples from their own classrooms to make suggestions about language arts instruction and argue for particular instructional approaches or ideas, and leaders pick up their suggestions. Follower-leader interactions focus on pedagogical knowledge and instructional resources.

If we sat in on one of the leadership routines related to mathematics, however, we would observe very different interactions among leaders, as well as between leaders and followers. Consider a mathematics professional development meeting for seventeen K–3 teachers led by a first-grade teacher and a third-grade teacher, two of the four teacher leaders for mathematics at Adams School. At this particular meeting (typical for Adams), there are no administrators present. At the outset, each teacher is given a folder with mathematics activities that they can use in their classrooms. The two leaders gathered these materials from some books they reviewed, which they then summarized for the teachers present. One of the mathematics leaders described some strategies and questions, picked up from a book she had read, that teachers might use in their mathematics lessons. She encouraged the teachers to use the book, explaining that it "gives you . . . some things you can do," and "it doesn't involve worksheets; the children get to write and explain and do problem solving." The second mathematics leader pointed out that having students write and explain is especially important in preparing them for the "open-ended items on the ISAT." She then brought two other books to teachers' attention. One includes numerous games that teachers can use in their mathematics classrooms, while the other focuses on linking mathematics and literacy instruction. She went on to identify a number of other books for teachers. Later, the first mathematics leader described an activity for teaching students about shapes and pointed out that students need to know shapes "when they take the ISAT." The second mathematics leader pointed out that this particular activity is consistent with the standards set by the National Council of Teachers of Mathematics in 2000. Teachers interrupted occasionally to clarify or ask for more specific information: "What grade level is this program for?" "I am wondering if there's anything special you've seen for special needs kids?" The two leaders' actions are relatively similar; both identified resources, presented pedagogical knowledge, and used ISAT and NCTM standards to motivate teachers to use particular instructional strategies.

Mathematics-related leadership practice contrasts with literacy-related leadership practice in at least four ways:

- In mathematics-related leadership practice, leaders tend to play parallel roles, whereas in literacy-related leadership practice, leaders play different roles as well as similar ones.

- Followers have much less to say in mathematics-related leadership practice in comparison with literacy-related leadership practice.

- When followers do talk in mathematics-related leadership activities, they mostly acknowledge that they understand and agree with what leaders are presenting or ask for clarification.

- In mathematics-related leadership activities, knowledge and ideas come almost entirely from the leaders, who rely chiefly on external sources of expertise such as books and other programs.

The subject matter makes a difference in the practice of school leadership. These subject matter differences reflect the distinctive social norms that have evolved in different subject areas in schools and in their broader institutional environments—universities, state and federal policy environments, textbook publishing, and testing companies.

Followers are central to leadership practice, though in different ways in language arts and in mathematics. While the interactions among leaders shape leadership practice, they do so in interaction with followers. In how they interact with leaders, followers help define leadership practice.

The Situation Dimension

Most people recognize that the situation is critical to all sorts of practice, including leadership practice. The situation of practice can make it more or less difficult. Repairing an electrical plug with a kitchen knife rather than a screwdriver slows the work and often undermines its quality. However, aspects of the situation do more than quicken and smarten up our execution or performance of some preset plan of action.

Tools, routines, structures, and other aspects of the situation often serve as go-betweens in our interactions with others in and on the world. Aspects of the situation mediate our interactions, and in these interactions, practice takes shape. In this way, the situation defines practice in interaction with leaders and followers. Aspects of the situation, realized in leadership practice, do not simply influence practice from the outside in by enabling people to execute their plans of action more or less efficiently. Instead, they give form to leadership practice in interaction with leaders and followers. Tools and routines and other aspects of the situation put some elements of the interactions at the forefront while downplaying or ignoring others. They thereby help define what leaders and followers must be heedful of and how heedful they must be. By way of example, consider two different versions of the teacher evaluation protocol, a tool common to leadership work in many schools. Protocol A includes a checklist of teaching behaviors or processes such as wait time and use of praise. The checklist in protocol B focuses on academic work such as the cognitive complexity of the mathematical tasks and how students justified their mathematical ideas. In interactions between leaders and followers, protocol A puts different aspects of teaching in the forefront compared with protocol B. In this way, different teacher evaluation tools can contribute to defining leadership practice differently. Hence, new or redesigned tools may change practice, just as we hope that new knowledge and skill on the part of leaders might change that practice. The situation is also a product of the interactions among leaders and followers. Thus, it is both the medium for and the outcome of leadership practice.

The Situation: Tools, Routines, and the List Goes On

From a distributed perspective, the challenge involves not only identifying those aspects of the situation that enable and constrain leadership practice but also capturing how they shape that practice. After considering what might fall into the category of situation in this section, I organize the remainder of this chapter around two cases from the Distributed Leadership Study. These cases focus on just two aspects of the situation—tools and routines. There are many other aspects of the situation that merit consideration—structures, culture, language, and so on—but those are for another book. The same dynamics captured in my discussion of tools and routines hold for other aspects of the situation.

Administrators and teachers can create their own tools and routines. School leaders design some of their own tools and routines locally to meet the particular needs of their school. The Breakfast Club at Adams School is a good example (Halverson, 2002). But tools and routines are not always built locally. Other tools and routines, such as the school improvement planning process, come ready-made from the district office, the state or national government, or some other external provider and are received by school leaders. School leaders also inherit tools and routines from previous administrations when they take responsibility for a new school or department. These tools and routines often preceded a new leader's tenure and may have been staples of doing business in a school for decades. Finally, tools and routines can be appropriated by leaders and followers from one situation and adapted to serve some new purpose.

The Writing Folder Review: A Case of Routines and Tools

Principal Cathy Nelson is a twenty-year veteran of the principal's office at Hillside School on Chicago's South Side. Monitoring instruction has been "a big priority" for her, and one or two classroom observations are typically part of her daily routine. She also uses the routine of the writing folder review to monitor instruction and lead improvement in writing instruction.[7]

Nelson, whose energy and presence offers no hint of her imminent retirement, was firmly committed to improving opportunities for Hillside's predominantly Mexican American student population to succeed academically. She was convinced that the ability to write and communicate clearly was critical to the success of Mexican American students. Over the past decade, she has taken on this challenge, focusing particularly on improving writing instruction. Central to her efforts was her monthly review of students' writing folders. Nelson appropriated the writing folder process as a leadership routine and tool.

The writing folder review was an outcome of leadership practice. It evolved out of Nelson's attempt to address the fact that Hillside students were not good writers because formal writing instruction was neither regular nor systematic. Appropriating the writing folder to leverage change in writing instruction, Nelson and the Hillside teachers built a new leadership routine at Hillside and redefined the writing folder from a simple instructional tool to a leadership tool.

From October through April, Hillside teachers agreed to submit a monthly folder that contained one composition written by each student in their class. Nelson described it this way: "I write notes to every single classroom every single month. . . . I try to have it be constructive criticism. I try to give specific things that maybe the class might want to work on." Based on her reading of each student's writing samples, Nelson provided the teachers and students with written feedback. She offered specific guidance about the teaching of writing, identifying skills they should cover and commenting on teachers' grading of students' work. In her comments to students, she praised their writing and pointed out areas that needed more work.

The writing folder review routine enabled Nelson to monitor what was going on in writing instruction at Hillside School each month. She explained, "I can tell a lot of what's happening in the classroom by just reading folders and providing feedback to teachers. I can see people who maybe need to work a little on certain things." Through her written feedback to both students and teachers about the teaching and learning of writing in each classroom, she was able to identify weaknesses in terms of what was being covered in writing instruction and what counted as good work. Through her comments, she was also able to work on motivating both teachers and students to improve writing instruction.

The writing folder review routine is now institutionalized at Hillside School. Both school leaders and teachers take it seriously. Teachers turn in their writing folders, Nelson reads them and provides written feedback to teachers and students, and teachers and students read the comments and work to address the issues identified by their principal. Nelson commented, "It forced teachers to actually teach writing as a subject and not just as a homework assignment and encouraged them to use the writing as an integrated thing, not as a stand-alone." Hillside teachers reported that the writing folder routine influenced their teaching. Mandy Crawford described how it has changed her approach to writing instruction: "I switch my whole day around so they get almost an hour to work on [writing]. . . . I have received notes from Mrs. Nelson. We have to turn in compositions monthly. . . . But . . . what I've had to change in my approach this year is giving them more time to think, more time to work, more time to review the process. You know, review the criteria. You have to have this, this, and this."[8]

Leadership practice took shape in the interaction of Nelson, the teachers, the students, and the writing folder as a key leadership routine and tool. The writing folder tool shaped leadership practice in a number of ways. First, it focused the interactions among Nelson, the students, and the teachers on what students were learning (or not learning) about writing and on what teachers were really teaching rather than on teachers' claims about what they had taught. In other words, the writing folder focused what leaders and followers were heedful of in their interactions on what students could actually write. Second, the writing folder framed the interactions so that Nelson could provide feedback to students and teachers simultaneously, motivating and engaging both in efforts to improve writing instruction. This was unlike typical efforts to change teaching that neglect students and focus exclusively on the teacher. Students, by virtue of their motivation to write and their willingness to put in the effort to produce text, fundamentally shape classroom instruction.

Leadership practice at Hillside might easily have used other tools to improve writing instruction. The leadership practice might have involved Nelson interacting with teachers based on a series of model writing lessons or discussions of teachers' lesson plans. Or Nelson and the teachers might have interacted based on a set of monitoring sheets that teachers filled out each marking period, recording the writing skills covered during that period. But if different tools had been used, the interactions and the leadership practice would have been different. A routine such as a monthly review of teachers' lesson plans, for example, would have been much more likely to focus the interactions on teachers' content coverage. It would not have connected directly with students or focused on what they actually learned. The selection and development of tools matters for leadership because they enable and constrain different practices. Tools like the writing folder generate different and distinct types of data that people have to be heedful of in their interactions. Lesson plans and other tools would generate different data.

Focusing on the products of writing instruction—students' writing—the writing folder tool was less likely to frame the interactions among Nelson and her staff on strategies for teaching writing. Because the routine focused on one-on-one interactions between Nelson, the teachers, and the students, it was also less likely to enable interactions among teachers about their writing instruction. The writing folder review illustrates how the situation defines leadership practice and is a product of that practice. The writing folder case also illustrates how even when a single leader is the primary mover and shaker in the execution of a leadership routine, the distributed framework can still be used to understand the practice.

Student Test Data: A Case of Leadership Tools

Standardized student achievement tests are a widely used tool in schools. Teachers often complain that they limit or constrain or even distort their teaching practice. Many school and system leaders claim the contrary, arguing that achievement tests press teachers to pay attention to the achievement of all students. The test tool shapes classroom and leadership practices. But tests can also be hijacked, modified, or used differently than their designers intended; they can be influenced and altered by leadership practice.

The student achievement data generated by standardized tests are also a tool. In schools in the Distributed Leadership Study, achievement data were a widely used tool. The school district's policies held schools accountable for student achievement as measured by the Iowa Test of Basic Skills (ITBS). Student performance on the ITBS at benchmark grades became the district's primary measure of school accountability and progress. The key sanction was probation for low performance. In 1996, for example, the school district put 109 elementary schools (20 percent) on probation because fewer than 15 percent of their students performed at or above national norms on the reading and mathematics sections of the ITBS (Hess, 2000). Furthermore, beginning with the 1996–97 school year, students who failed to achieve at a certain level on the ITBS would have to attend summer school. If they still failed to achieve at the required level at the end of summer school, they would not be promoted to the next grade level. Thus, test data got the attention of school leaders, teachers, and students in Chicago schools. These district-level routines—putting schools on probation, not promoting students who failed to meet a certain level of competency—shaped how test data figured in school leadership practice.

As a tool, student achievement data were prominently featured in many leadership routines, including professional development workshops, faculty meetings, literacy and mathematics committees, and school improvement planning. Test score data framed the practice of these routines by focusing leaders' and followers' interactions on what students were able to do and not able to do in mathematics and literacy. Test score data defined leadership practice by focusing the interactions on content coverage and, in many cases, test preparation. At Upton School, for example, professional development meetings—a key leadership routine for instruction—focused on skills tested in language arts, skills tested in mathematics, constructing multiple-choice test items, and preparing students for the ITBS. Typically, school leaders interpreted the student achievement data, identifying areas in which students had not done well and highlighting those in which students had done miserably. They then presented their findings to staff as priorities for the next school year. In this way, the tool shaped the interactions among leaders and followers.

While the tool framed interactions in all schools, the tool was also transformed in leadership practice granted in some schools more than others. The extent to which and how the achievement data tool was transformed depended on the school. The situation at Baxter Elementary School is illustrative.

At Baxter School, both leaders and teachers viewed student achievement data on the ITBS as an integral tool for leading instructional improvement in mathematics and language arts. Baxter staff had little reason to fret over student test scores and district accountability levers; the school had met national norms in core subject areas at each of the benchmark grade levels (third, fifth, and eighth) for at least five years and had received national recognition for academic excellence. It was acknowledged in the city as one of the best schools. Still, formal and informal leaders at Baxter used disaggregated test score data as a barometer for measuring school improvement and as a means to build support for sustaining efforts to improve instruction. Lance Stern, described by both himself and his staff as "very much of a data guy," conducted regular longitudinal analyses of Baxter students' achievement on the ITBS, identifying trends across time by grade level and by cohort. He generated numerous graphs of these trends and used these graphs to focus and frame discussions among leaders and teachers about the nature of problems at the school, as well as possible solutions to them. Stern and his leadership team went to great lengths to repackage standardized test data in order to engage teachers.

Stern's customized tools framed the interactions among leaders and followers at Baxter differently than if they had just relied on the data as they had been received from the district office. After all, compared with other Chicago schools, Baxter was doing very well; in that sense, there was no problem with the instructional program. With respect to his longitudinal analysis, Stern explained, "The analysis made clear that . . . Baxter was either at the bottom or really close to the bottom, in terms of the amount of actual growth that students were making. Forget about where the growth started! Forget about the base! Forget about the end! Just, you know, how many months of progress, on an average, were sixth graders achieving at Baxter School between 1991 and 1995?" Hence, at Baxter, student assessment data—a received tool from the district office— were transformed within and through the leadership practice that repackaged and revised it. These transformed tools reframed the interactions among leaders and among leaders and followers in the performance of leadership routines such as the leadership team meetings and grade-level meetings. Simply put, these tools focused the interactions on defining and solving problems with Baxter's instructional program rather than on merely celebrating success. In this way, student assessment data as a tool was an outcome of leadership practice at Baxter while also defining that practice in interaction with leaders and followers.

But there is even more going on at Baxter in regard to student achievement data. Over the past decade, Stern and his leadership team have worked to build an elaborate infrastructure of routines and committee structures in order to engage teachers, along with formal leaders, in the work of leadership. This infrastructure includes a faculty leadership group, bimonthly grade-level meetings, and subcommittees for literacy, mathematics, and science. These routines and committee structures, along with a culture in which teachers are expected to engage in decision making, provide an infrastructure for defining instructional problems and constructing solutions to these problems.

At Baxter, student test data are not treated simply as a blueprint to improve test scores but also as one source of information to help school staff identify problems and construct solutions to them. In leadership practices at the school, teachers work with student achievement data to identify trends, combining them with other information to develop solutions to problems they have identified. Discussion of test score data has become a regular feature in leadership routines from grade-level meetings to leadership team meetings. At one faculty meeting, an observer noted:

> When I entered the auditorium, Rene motioned me to several neat piles of materials on the auditorium stage. These were the materials for the meeting. . . . The materials display detailed information on student outcomes, but the charts [which, I learned later, Mr. Stern had developed and which were a mainstay of meetings he organized] were easy to read, with labels for those of us who had difficulty with numbers and charts. Different kinds of data were displayed on different kinds of charts, and each chart has its own color. The first chart was already up on the screen—projected by the overhead that I assumed Mr. Stern would use for his presentation.

At Baxter, the test data tool is not just used to boost pride but is embedded in routines and structures that frame interactions among leaders and teachers so that they can figure out the roots of instructional problems and build solutions to them.

Student test data help define leadership practice. In some schools, this tool has been redefined in leadership practice and as a result of these transformations has shaped leadership practice differently.

Conclusion

If you take a distributed perspective, the practice of leadership has to be the central concern. Leadership roles, functions, and structures are important. But leadership practice is paramount. It is the holy grail. A distributed perspective offers a very particular way of thinking about leadership practice. It does not equate leadership practice with the actions of individual leaders. The actions of school leaders are important but still only one of the elements that contribute to defining leadership practice. We have to go further than the leader-plus aspect.

Interactions, as distinct from actions, are critical. Interactions are the key to unlocking leadership practice from a distributed perspective. Leadership practice takes shape in the interactions of leaders, followers, and their situation. This approach contrasts with the leader-plus approach, in which the concern is identifying leaders and specifying their actions. From a distributed perspective, simply counting up the actions of leaders will not be sufficient on its own; the whole is more than the sum of the parts. Hence, in a distributed approach, we have to start with the leadership practice, observe it, infer who the leaders are, and begin to explore the interactions among leaders, followers, and their situation.

From a distributed perspective, leaders can interact in the co-performance of leadership routines even when they seek different or conflicting outcomes. Working together on a leadership routine does not necessarily mean working toward similar goals. The situation is critical in the distributed perspective on leadership practice. Tools and routines are the vehicles through which leaders interact with one another and with followers. Routines and tools provide scripts that capture repeated patterns for these interactions. However, in actual practice, a routine or use of a particular tool can be modified and revised. As a result, the scripts for routines and tools are changed. Tools that were designed for one purpose can take on a new purpose through practice.

Research that uses the practice aspect of the distributed framework to understand school leadership is scarce. Much work remains to be done in building theories, generating tenable hypotheses, and testing hypotheses. This work poses some major challenges. One challenge concerns the identification of leadership practice in schools. Simply relying on what formally designated leaders do is inadequate, because leadership practice occurs in interactions involving formal leaders, informal leaders, and followers, as well as their situation. A second challenge involves the development of valid and reliable methods for documenting leadership practice once it is identified. Shifting the focus from an exclusive focus on the actions of leaders to the *interactions* in leadership practice poses major methodological puzzles for scholars and practitioners.

Notes

1. For a more detailed analysis of this and other literacy committee meetings at Adams School, see Jennifer Sherer's doctoral dissertation in progress, School of Education and Social Policy, Northwestern University, Evanston, IL.

2. My initial foray into characterizing the nature of interactions among leaders relied chiefly on work on interdependencies (Spillane, Diamond, and Jita, 2000, 2003).

3. Building on Thompson's work, Malone and others (1999) suggest three types of dependencies arising from resources that are related to multiple activities:

   - *Sharing dependencies* occur when multiple activities all use the same resource.

   - *Fit dependencies* arise when multiple activities collectively produce a single resource.

   - *Flow dependencies* arise when one activity produces a resource that is used by another activity.

4. I thank Michael Cohen and Jane Dutton for drawing my attention to work on heedfulness.

5. Gronn (2003) offers a slightly different typology involving definitions of *co-performance* and *collective performance*, which are roughly analogous to what I term *collaborated distribution* and *collective distribution*, respectively. Gronn's typology focuses both on the types of distribution and their origins. *Spontaneous collaboration* refers to impromptu collaborations that are frequently transient and motivated by particular challenges. *Intuitive understanding* refers to working relationships that develop over time as two or more people work together and learn to trust and rely on one another. Finally, through design and adaptation, new structures enable two or more individuals to co-perform.

6. I thank Bill Firestone for pressing me to attend to situations in which leaders pull in opposing directions during the pilot phase of the Distributed Leadership Study.

7. For a detailed analysis of the writing folder routine and tool, see Coldren and Spillane, 2005; Spillane, Sherer, and Coldren, in press.

8. Other teachers at Hillside provided similar testimony.

4

A Distributed Perspective on
and in Leadership Practice

W e need a new way of thinking about leadership. The distributed perspective offers one. It offers a way of approaching the very practical problems of school leadership. Moreover, it provides a way of thinking systematically about the *practice* of leadership.

Distributed leadership takes a stance with respect to what is important in understanding school leadership. However, it does not prescribe what we ought to do in order to practice leadership more effectively, to produce certain outcomes. What distributed leadership, like all leadership theory, can do to benefit practice is provide a frame that helps school leaders and others interpret and reflect on practice as a basis for rethinking and revising it. In this way, a distributed leadership approach can be a powerful tool for transforming the practice of leadership. It cannot, however, provide a blueprint for how to practice (Argyris and Schön, 1974; Schön, 1988). In the words of Hughes and Busch (1991), "Theories are most useful for influencing practice when they suggest new ways in which events and situations can be perceived" (p. 103). Hence, a distributed perspective may have practical entailments as well as entailments for how we understand practice.

Getting Practical

Thinking about leadership from a distributed perspective is essential. Individuals who single-handedly try to lead complex organizations like schools set themselves up for failure. Getting beyond the heroic plot is imperative. A distributed perspective makes it possible for the work of leadership to be manageable. Rita Johnson, the principal at Kelly School on Chicago's West Side, commented, "Initially, I tried to do it all. I was trying to do it all, and that was impossible. You cannot be all things to all people. . . . I don't know everything about everything, and I have people on staff; all the staff members help, but I rely heavily on my assistant principal that at one time was a classroom teacher. . . . I rely on my computer teacher, the counselor, Ms. P. (a full-time teacher). I rely on the whole staff, but these people are sort of key—'cause every administration has some key people." As Johnson points out, one person cannot do it all. There is too much involved in leading a school, even a small school like Kelly that has fewer than three hundred students.

The issue here is not just having sufficient bodies to do the work of school leadership. There is more. Johnson's comment, "I don't know everything about everything," says it. It is unrealistic to expect any school principal to know everything about leading complex organizations like schools.

A cursory analysis of the work of school leadership suggests that the knowledge one might be expected to master is extensive. Let us look at the core work, though it is only one aspect, of school leadership: leading improvement in teaching and learning. A quick inventory indicates that school leaders need to know something about content knowledge, pedagogical knowledge, curricular knowledge, knowledge about students, and knowledge about adult learning. They also need to have some level of competence not just in a single subject area but in several, so that they can make wise choices about hiring teachers, facilitate the selection of curricular materials, observe instruction, and make informed judgments about its quality. This is all too much for one person. Even expecting two or three people to master all of this expertise might still be setting expectations too high. But we have to attend to more than the leader-plus aspect.

Getting to Practice

We can get practical but still never get to practice. That would be most unfortunate! Leadership improvement will ultimately depend on the day-to-day practice of leadership in schools. New structures and new roles can change leadership in a school. But structures, roles, or even the expertise of leaders can change while the day-to-day practice of leadership remains the same. One of the greatest challenges that education will face over the next several decades is understanding leadership practice as a basis for thinking about its improvement.

The distributed perspective shifts the focus from leaders to leadership practice. In this way, efforts to understand school leadership are firmly anchored in the practice of leadership. Leadership roles, structures, and functions are still important. But from a distributed perspective, leadership practice is the vital concern. The distributed perspective offers a particular way of thinking about leadership practice, arguing that practice gets defined in the interactions of leaders, followers, and their situation. This framing differs from conventional accounts in which practice is typically equated with the actions of a practitioner and seen as a function of the practitioner's knowledge (or lack thereof).

For practitioners, the ultimate test of any framework for examining practice is whether it contributes to understanding leadership *in* practice. Leadership practice in particular schools is where the rubber meets the road for distributed leadership. Distributed leadership can be a diagnostic tool for reflecting *on* leadership practice. It can also be a design tool for thinking about the improvement of leadership practice.

A Distributed Perspective on Leadership Practice

The distributed perspective provides school leaders and those who work with them a set of analytical tools to support their reflection on leadership practice. The distributed framework can serve as a diagnostic tool for assessing leadership in schools that takes us directly to leadership practice—the day-to-day work of leading a school. As a diagnostic device, the distributed perspective, beginning with the leader-plus aspect, presses us to investigate the *leadership routines* in the lived reality as well as in the formal structure of a school. Such an investigation might explore the following questions:

- What tasks or activities go into the execution of the routine?

- Who is responsible for the execution of these tasks?

- What tools are used in the execution of these tasks?

- What leadership functions and organizational goals are these routines designed to address or have they evolved to address over time?

In all of this, teaching and learning should be a central concern. Linking routines to leadership functions (for example, selling a vision) is not sufficient. We need to determine whether and how routines connect with teaching and learning. These connections can be either direct or indirect. For example, in the case of the Breakfast Club routine, discussed in Chapter Three, there are both direct and indirect connections between the leadership routine and instruction. The Breakfast Club connects directly with teaching by providing opportunities for teachers to learn about teaching. At the same time, the Breakfast Club routine is indirectly connected to instruction because it is designed to build opportunities for teachers to collaborate about their teaching in an effort to build and sustain a professional community. As a routine designed to build professional community—and there is evidence that it has been successful in this regard—the Breakfast Club works indirectly on teaching by making the conditions of teachers' work more supportive of teacher learning.

Leadership routines can connect with teaching and learning in a variety of ways; teachers are not the only avenues from leadership practice to instructional practice. The writing folder review routine at Hillside School, for example, connects with instruction through teachers and also through students. Some leadership routines connect with teaching chiefly or exclusively through students. The Real Men Read routine at two of the Distributed Leadership Study sites, for example, is designed to motivate black male students to read by creating opportunities in which black male adults read aloud to students. The theory behind this routine is that if students are shown that reading is a cool activity, even for men, they will be more willing to read and, as a result, more engaged in reading instruction. Understanding how leadership practice connects with instructional practice is essential. Relationships between leadership practice and instructional practice also vary by subject area. Hence, in any effort to understand leadership routines in a school, sensitivity to instructional differences between curricular domains is essential.

Attending to the practice aspect of distributed leadership extends the diagnostic work and presses us to ask further questions about the performance of the routine:

- How do leaders co-practice a particular leadership routine?

- How do followers mutually constitute this practice?

- How do aspects of the situation frame interactions among leaders and among leaders and followers in this practice?

Understanding the interactions among leaders in the co-practice of particular routines is important. One issue concerns the knowledge and expertise needed for the execution of the routine. Specifically, we must consider how knowledge and expertise are distributed among those who co-perform a leadership routine, asking whether essential knowledge is missing that might improve the practice.

The affective and motivational dimensions of the interactions must also be taken into account in analyzing the co-practice of leadership routines. With respect to motivation, we have to take into account the collective by examining whether the group dynamic enhances or constrains motivation. Individuals' motivation may differ, depending on the person with whom they are co-performing. Effort is not entirely an individual attribute; it is also influenced by the people with whom we work. One might extend considerable effort while working with one set of colleagues but very little effort while working with a different group.

With respect to followers, the distributed perspective urges us to observe how followers' participation in a leadership routine contributes to defining leadership practice. Noticing patterns of follower participation—not only how frequently they participate but also the roles they play when they participate and the substance of their participation—will help us understand how followers contribute to the construction of leadership practice. Comparing and contrasting followers' and leaders' interactions across different routines and across the same routine in different school subjects is one potentially useful strategy.

With respect to the situation, the distributed perspective presses us to move beyond the identification of aspects of the situation that matter. We must ask how aspects of the situation, such as the tools used in the performance of a routine, contribute to defining the interactions among leaders and among leaders and followers. Hence, practitioners should ask how particular tools frame the interactions among leaders and among leaders and followers. A helpful strategy is to consider how alternative tools might frame the interactions differently. We might even consider actually changing the tool used in a particular routine and exploring whether and how the interactions change in the process. For example, by supplanting the research articles commonly used during Breakfast Club meetings at Adams School with samples of students' work in language arts or mathematics, we might tease apart how an aspect of the situation focuses the interactions among leaders and followers.

A Distributed Perspective in Leadership Practice: Design Principles

The distributed perspective can also serve as a design tool for school leaders, providing a set of ideas that can be used to inform their design decisions. Ordinarily, we think of design work as the purview of architects and inventors, but it is an everyday enterprise that many of us pursue in some form or other. "Design refers to the human endeavor of shaping objects to purposes" (Perkins, 1986, pp. 1–2). Design typically is not a one-time event, involving a series of plans and resulting in a product that is implemented more widely. Instead, design usually is an ongoing process whereby something like a leadership routine is constantly being tweaked so that it more adequately meets a particular purpose. Sometimes we undertake major or modest adjustments to a routine or tool so that it can serve some new purpose. Design also occurs through social evolution. Design can be thought of, then, as a continual, sometimes conscious and explicit process of adopting and adapting things for particular purposes. Indeed, school leaders are often rebuilding, if not building, the proverbial plane as they fly it. Design and redesign are central in the work of leadership.

As a design tool, the distributed perspective offers a particular way of thinking about school leadership. At least three design principles are central:

> *Principle One:* The *practice* of leadership should be a central focus in efforts to improve school leadership because it is a more proximal cause of instructional improvement than leadership roles, processes, or structures.

Principle Two: Intervening to improve leadership necessitates attention to *interactions*, not just actions, because leadership practice takes shape in the interactions among leaders and followers.

Principle Three: Intervening to improve leadership practice requires attention to the design and redesign of aspects of the *situation*, such as routines and tools, because the situation helps define leadership practice.

In an effort not to repeat myself, I will not elaborate on each of these design principles; the preceding chapters offer considerable elaboration. As a design tool, the distributed framework enables practitioners to specify a set of design principles to guide leadership practice and efforts to improve that practice.

Specifically, the distributed framework offers practitioners a set of diagnostic and design tools, enabling them to stand back and reflect on how leadership is distributed in their school. Like any analytical tool, it frames the phenomenon under scrutiny—leadership in this case—in a particular manner, highlighting some aspects of the phenomenon and downgrading or even altogether obscuring other aspects. What is important in adopting a particular frame, such as the distributed leadership frame advanced in this book, is that we don't forget that we are using it and we remember which features of the phenomenon under study it highlights and how it highlights them. We could use a different framework or lens—such as individual cognition—and, in doing so, see leadership differently.

Lessons from Practice, for Practice

In arguing that distributed leadership is descriptive before it is prescriptive, I am not suggesting that prescriptions are at odds with taking a distributed perspective on and in leadership practice. Furthermore, I am not arguing that distributed leadership as a descriptive framework is norm-free. As I discussed earlier, it is no more or less agnostic than commonly used theoretical frameworks in the hard sciences and the not-so-hard social sciences. The distributed leadership perspective as outlined in this book in and of itself is not a recipe for effective leadership practice. Rather, it offers a productive way of thinking about leadership both from a diagnostic and a design perspective. Furthermore, it offers scholars a conceptual framework for studying leadership, as I will discuss further in the rest of this chapter. Considering the current knowledge base, we should be wary of those who peddle versions of distributed leadership as a tonic to cure all that ails schools. If distributed leadership is a tonic, its curing powers will have much more to do with how it is used by practitioners and those who work with them on improving leadership than with simply swallowing the approach in its entirety.

At any rate, I am convinced that the continued systematic application of the distributed framework to the study of leadership will lead to the identification of patterns in how leadership is distributed in schools. Furthermore, I believe that it can and will lead over time to causal inferences about the relationship between how leadership is distributed and instructional improvement in terms of student learning. Based on my ongoing analysis of data from the Distributed Leadership Study, I offer two lessons from practice for leadership practice:

Strategic decision making in designing leadership practice must be ongoing. Taking a distributed perspective means that by definition leadership is distributed in schools, although how it is distributed differs, depending on the school and leadership routine, among other things. A good starting assumption is that leadership practice is distributed. The challenge for school leadership then concerns how leadership is distributed—the extent to which leadership is distributed in different routines, who is involved in the coperformance of various routines, and how the situation defines leadership practice.

Design and redesign are central to leadership work. Cathy Nelson's writing folder, Lance Stern's graphs on student achievement, and Brenda Williams and her team's Breakfast Club are but a few of the examples from schools in the Distributed Leadership Study of routines that are constantly being tweaked and adapted in order to improve instructional practice. Attending strategically to how leadership is distributed in a school involves ongoing design *and* redesign.

At Adams School, the distribution of leadership for instruction was not left to chance. Brenda Williams, the literacy coordinator, and other leaders at Adams deliberately involved others in leadership tasks, strategically distributing leadership among leaders and classroom teachers. However, the distribution of leadership among formally designated leaders and teachers was not accomplished through declarations from the principal's office that anointed teachers and administrators as leaders for particular routines. Instead, it was done through the design of the routines, which included decisions to create leadership positions, strategically fill those positions with both administrators and teachers, and build infrastructures that enabled administrators and teachers to perform leadership work. As Williams explained, "I created a situation where teachers can evolve in leadership roles within a school, and they like that, and when they evolve in that leadership role, they know that I trust them to do what it is that they are doing." However, Williams and her leadership team also acted strategically when it came to developing teachers as leaders. Simply appointing teachers to leadership positions and creating structures that enabled them to assume leadership responsibilities were insufficient. At Adams School, administrators identified teachers with leadership potential and provided them with professional development opportunities to hone their skills, scaffolding their transition into leadership positions. Moreover, in hiring new teachers, Adams's leaders again acted strategically in looking not just for good classroom teachers but also for teachers who had leadership potential and who could therefore address some of the school's leadership needs.

At Adams School, design was ongoing, and redesign of the existing infrastructure was constant. For example, Adams's leaders constantly tweaked and adapted the Breakfast Club routine both to better fit its original purpose and to address new purposes. Putting new routines and tools in place is just one part of the leadership design challenge; another part involves ensuring through ongoing design and redesign that the routines and tools meet the purposes they are intended to support. Routines evolve at some times through the explicit redesign decisions of school administrators and teachers and at other times through a gradual process of social evolution.

Design without diagnosis is a recipe for disaster. While design is critical, careful diagnostic work is equally important. When Brenda Williams arrived as the principal at Adams School, all was not well: fewer than 20 percent of the students were scoring at or above national norms in reading, and teachers worked mainly as isolates, rarely talking with one another about their work. Still, Williams did not rush in with new designs to remedy all that ailed Adams School. Instead, she began by trying to get a handle on the situation at Adams. She related, "I came in February, so I had four or five months to really get a sense of what was going on." Williams's efforts to make sense of what was going on at Adams addressed everything from staff politics to the particulars of instruction at specific grade levels. She explained, "One of the big issues . . . as I moved from classroom to classroom and as I looked at lesson plans, [was that] there were totally different learning experiences going on for the children." Before Williams and her team set about any major redesign of the leadership infrastructure at Adams School, she took careful stock of how things already worked at Adams.

Contrast Williams's transition into the principal's office at Adams School with Lin Koh's transition into the principalship at Kosten School. When Koh arrived at Kosten School in the middle of the year, she had little information to go on, for the old administration had destroyed all formal records of school policies and procedures. Consequently, as Koh put it, "We're really starting from the bottom." She acknowledged the difficulty: "It's hard when there's a history of things . . . and you don't know anything about it." The chairperson of the local school council echoed this account, noting that Koh "came into a school were there were no records, where there was no structure, and she had to create it, from scratch." That is exactly what Koh set out to do. She immediately designed a new infrastructure for managing instruction and its improvement at Kosten. She put in place a variety of new routines that were designed to hold teachers accountable for teaching the district's prescribed standards. In the process, she disrupted business as usual at Kosten.

As one might anticipate, many teachers passively and actively resisted these new designs. A fifth-grade teacher at Kosten captured the situation: "I am not sure if they [Koh and her assistant principal] are giving enough time to get a feel for things before they just jump into things. I think they have very good ideas, but they might be moving too fast." Koh failed to take the time to get a handle on how things were done at Kosten, from staff politics to the way teachers received guidance for instruction. Granted, this was a difficult challenge, considering that the previous administration had destroyed most of the records and that she took the helm at Kosten in midyear. Still, she could have taken some time to figure out how things were done at Kosten—the lived organization—before designing a new infrastructure for instruction. Instead, she rushed in with new designs without diagnosing the landscape in which her designs would have to take root and grow. While Koh attempted to change course a year into her tenure, for many teachers it was too late; in their eyes, she already lacked creditability with staff. Design that is not based on careful diagnosis can undermine efforts to transform leadership practice.

Developing Leadership Practice

A distributed perspective challenges the preoccupation with leader development, urging greater attention to the development of leadership practice. Many programs for preparation and development in educational administration have an exclusive concern with the development of leaders, which more often than not is equated with principals' knowledge and skills. The assumption here is that if individuals learn new knowledge and skills, they will be able to act in new and more effective ways. However, improved leadership practice does not necessarily follow from improved knowledge and skills, because leadership practice and the actions of individual leaders are not one and the same.

If leadership practice takes shape in the interactions among leaders and followers—that is, if it is more than the actions of individual leaders—then it seems wise to think about the challenge of school leadership development as one of developing the practice of leadership rather than thinking exclusively in terms of developing school principals. Development efforts are more likely to be successful if they work on interactions rather than focus exclusively on the actions of any one leader, because the actions of the principal or any other leader are not the only elements that give shape to leadership practice. Anchoring the leadership preparation and development challenge in leadership practice could involve principal preparation programs that work to develop a distributed mindset, helping principals to think about leadership practice and to think about it from a distributed perspective.

A distributed perspective also urges us to define the leadership preparation and development challenge as involving more than just programs for school principals. This perspective takes us beyond what individual leaders know and forces us to look at what expertise different leaders in a school bring to leadership work. However, the practice aspect suggests that the notion of expertise is more complex. We have to look at the collective interactions as well as the specific people in these interactions. A new approach to leadership expertise is essential. From a distributed perspective, expertise is not simply a function of a leader's thought processes and mental schemata. Viewing skill and expertise exclusively as a function of individual traits, styles, and schemata obscures how leaders' work is a function of their interactions. Intervening to improve school leadership by focusing chiefly on building the knowledge of an individual formal leader in a school may not be the most optimal, nor the most effective use of resources. If expertise is distributed, then the school rather than the individual leader may be the most appropriate unit for thinking about the development of leadership expertise.

A distributed leadership perspective suggests that the development of leadership practice needs to involve careful attention to the situation—routines, tools, and other aspects. One development strategy here might involve providing leaders with a tool kit of routines and tools and helping them to use these tools in their actual practice. One important task in this program would be helping leaders hone their performance of these routines with these tools in practice, through observation and reflection on practice. A distributed perspective, however, suggests that more than merely passing out tools and routines to school leaders would be necessary. School leaders need to be more than savvy consumers of the latest off-the-shelf tools and routines. It is critical to develop leaders' skills as designers of routines and tools.

Cultivating a distributed mind-set in school leaders and nurturing their skills as designers would help leadership development programs move beyond an exclusive reliance on school leaders' mastery of context-neutral, task-generic templates designed to script leadership practice. Instead, scripts for routines and tools would be presented not as simple recipes for performance but as occasions for design and redesign in practice.

Leadership Policy

A comprehensive discussion of the implications of a distributed leadership perspective for education policy is beyond the scope of this book. The terrain is vast. In this section, I consider three implications of a distributed perspective for education policy, in the hope that each will illuminate how a distributed perspective on leadership might inform education policymaking.

Viewing leadership from a distributed perspective means that education policymakers must acknowledge that the work of leading schools involves more than the leadership of the school principal. Other leaders are critical, whether they be formally designated leaders such as assistant principals or teachers who take on leadership responsibilities. Hence, district policymakers need to consider how their policies on issues from leadership preparation and development to accountability reflect and support this reality. For example, do district policies, ranging from union contracts to teacher compensation, support or hinder teacher involvement in leadership work? While some school leaders can use a variety of means to engage teachers in the work of leadership, the challenge is greater if district policies fail to support such involvement on the part of teachers.

Another matter concerns district policies for assigning principals and other formally designated leaders to schools. To what extent does the school district have a strategy for assigning formally designated leaders to schools that takes account of the different sorts of expertise and skills of these leaders? Specifically, does the school district take a distributed perspective on leadership expertise and thus, in assigning different leaders to a school, work to ensure that the skills and expertise of the different leaders complement one another?

A related policy concern is leadership development. In most districts, leadership development programs focus on leader development and on school principals or those who aspire to such positions. From a distributed perspective, the exclusive focus on the school principal, coupled with the concentration on the individual leader rather than the school as the unit of intervention, is problematic. While principal preparation and development programs are important, it is also essential to create opportunities for other school leaders and other leadership teams to work together to improve leadership practice.

Conclusion

Some tout distributed leadership as a more effective approach to leading schools. Interestingly, many who take this stance have conducted no research on leadership from a distributed perspective. Others, working under the illusion that distributed leadership is a blueprint for leading schools, bemoan the weak empirical knowledge base on the effectiveness of distributed leadership as an approach to leadership. As I hope I have made clear in the preceding pages, I make no claims with respect to distributed leadership as a more or less effective approach to leading schools. Instead, I argue that distributed leadership, as I understand it, is a framework for thinking about and framing investigations of leadership practice. Application of this framework in studies of leadership will result in the generation of many tenable hypotheses that can be the subject of theory-testing studies. Figuring out the nature of the beast is imperative before making any attempts to measure its effects on teaching and student learning. More important, what is likely to be most salient is not the fact that leadership is distributed but *how* leadership is distributed.

The appeal of distributed leadership lies in the ease with which it can become all things to all people; various versions of distributed leadership have been associated with democratic leadership, participative leadership, collaborative leadership, and so on. As Alma Harris (2005) points out, there is a danger that distributed leadership will become a catch-all for any attempt to share leadership, transmit leadership, or delegate leadership to others. While that may be inevitable, it would be unfortunate in that distributed leadership as a perspective on leadership practice would end up being everything and nothing at the same time. A related problem is that in associating a distributed perspective on leadership with democratic and collaborative leadership, commentators frequently juxtapose it against more hierarchical and top-down approaches to leadership. As I have argued in this book, this is not my understanding of a distributed perspective on leadership. A distributed perspective on leadership can coexist with and be used beneficially to explore hierarchical and top-down leadership approaches.

Perhaps my greatest concern regarding a distributed perspective on leadership is the ease with which it can be subscribed to but not lived by in the practice of leadership, leadership development, and leadership scholarship. The heroics of leadership genre has a stranglehold on how we think about leadership. This emphasis reflects in part how the myth of individualism has captured our thinking about work in general and success in particular in Western society. Individualism is "a broadly perpetuated fiction in modern society" (Coleman, 1990, p. 300). Fiction indeed, but one that most of us find difficult to part with. In my view, to take a distributed perspective on leadership is not to lose sight of the individual but to acknowledge that leadership practice is defined in the interactions of leaders, followers, and their situation.

Distributed leadership in itself is not a recipe for effective leadership practice. Instead, it offers a productive way to think about leadership for both diagnostic and design purposes. A distributed framework is a means, through reflection and diagnosis, to more effective leadership practice. It also offers scholars a conceptual basis for studying leadership. A distributed perspective also urges us to define the leadership preparation and development challenge as involving more than just programs for school principals. Education policymakers who view leadership from a distributed perspective must acknowledge that the work of leading schools involves more than the leadership of the school principal.

Many observers agree that school leadership researchers, practitioners, and developers (including faculty in educational administration programs who prepare school leaders) have a crisis on hand. Specifically, the robustness of most empirical work on leadership is in doubt, many leadership preparation and development programs are deemed of poor quality, and school leaders report that these programs have little influence on their work. If we in the education field are to step up to the plate and take on the difficult challenges posed by this crisis, then new analytical or diagnostic tools that enable us to think about school leadership in fresh ways will be critical. The distributed perspective developed in this book offers such a tool, enabling us to approach school leadership in new ways that puts the *practice* of leadership center stage. In proposing the distributed perspective developed here as an analytical tool, I am not offering it as the holy grail for addressing all that ails the field of educational leadership; the field has far too many tools and approaches that are being marketed as the holy grail. I have more modest goals for the distributed perspective; I see it as a necessary tool in our tool kit as we rethink and rework school leadership.

References

Argyris, C., & Schön, D. A. (1974). *Theory in practice: Increasing professional effectiveness*. San Francisco: Jossey-Bass.

Ball, S. J. (1981). *Beachside comprehensive*. Cambridge, U.K.: Cambridge University Press.

Barnard, C. (1938). *The functions of the executive*. Cambridge, MA: Harvard University Press.

Bass, B. (1990). *Bass & Stogdill's handbook of leadership: Theory, research, and managerial applications*. New York: Free Press.

Bennett, N., Harvey, J. A., Wise, C., & Woods, P. A. (2003). *Distributed leadership: A desk study*. Retrieved from www.ncsl.org.uk/literature reviews

Bennis, W. G. (1959). Leadership theory and administrative behavior: The problems of authority. *Administrative Science Quarterly, 4*, 259–301.

Blase, J. J., & Blase, J. R. (1998). Principals, instructional leadership and teacher development: Teachers' perspectives. *Educational Administration Quarterly, 35*(3), 349–378.

Blase, J., & Kirby, P. (1992). *Bringing out the best in teachers: What effective principals do*. Thousand Oaks, CA: Corwin Press.

Bossert, S. T., Dwyer, D., Rowan, B., & Lee, G. V. (1982). The instructional management role of the principal. *Educational Administration Quarterly, 18*(3), 34–63.

Burns, J. M. (1978). *Leadership*. New York: HarperCollins.

Camburn, E., Rowan, B., & Taylor, J. (2003). Distributed leadership in schools: The case of elementary schools adopting comprehensive school reform models. *Educational Evaluation and Policy Analysis, 25*(4), 347–373.

Cochran-Smith, M., & Lytle, S. (Eds.). (1993). *Inside/outside: Teacher research and knowledge.* New York: Teachers College Press.

Cohen, D. K., & Ball, D. L. (1998). *Instruction, capacity, and improvement* (CPRE Research Report Series, RR-42). Philadelphia: Consortium for Policy Research in Education, University of Pennsylvania.

Coldren, A., & Spillane, J. (2005). *Making connections to teaching practice: Leadership for instruction in two urban schools.* Manuscript submitted for publication.

Coleman, J. (1990). *Foundations of social theory.* Cambridge, MA: Harvard University Press.

Copland, M. A. (2004). Leadership of inquiry: Building and sustaining capacity for school improvement. *Educational Evaluation and Policy Analysis, 25*(4), 375–396.

Crowther, F., Kaagan, S., Ferguson, M., & Hann, L. (2002). *Developing teacher leaders.* Thousand Oaks, CA: Corwin Press.

Cuban, L. (1988). *The managerial imperative and the practice of leadership in schools.* Albany: State University of New York Press.

Cyert, R. M., & March, J. G. (1963). *A behavioral theory of the firm.* Upper Saddle River, NJ: Prentice Hall.

Dahl, R. A. (1961). *Who governs? Democracy and power in an American city.* New Haven, CT: Yale University Press.

Eccles, R. G., & Nohria, N. (1992). *Beyond the hype: Rediscovering the essence of management.* Boston: Harvard Business School Press.

Feldman, M. S., & Pentland, B. T. (2003). Reconceptualizing organizational routines as a source of flexibility and change. *Administrative Science Quarterly, 48*(1), 94–118.

Fiedler, F. E. (1973). The contingency model: A reply to Ashour. *Organizational Behavior and Human Decision Processes, 9*(3), 356–368.

Firestone, W. A. (1979). Butte-Angels Camp: Conflict and transformation. In R. E. Herriott & N. Gross (Eds.), *The dynamics of planned educational change* (pp. 50–184). Berkeley, CA: McCutchan Press.

Firestone, W. A. (1989). Using reform: Conceptualizing district initiative. *Educational Evaluation and Policy Analysis, 11*(2), 151–165.

Goldring, E. B., & Rallis, S. F. (1993). *Principals of dynamic schools: Taking charge of change.* Newbury Park, CA: Corwin.

Goldstein, J. (2004). Making sense of distributed leadership: The case of peer assistance and review. *Educational Evaluation and Policy Analysis, 25*(4), 397–422.

Gronn, P. (2000). Distributed properties: A new architecture for leadership. *Educational Management & Administration, 28*(3), 317–338.

Gronn, P. (2002). *Distributed leadership as a unit of analysis. Leadership Quarterly, 13*(4), 423–451.

Gronn, P. (2003). *The new work of educational leaders: Changing leadership practice in an era of school reform.* London: Paul Chapman.

Grubb, W. N., Flessa, J., Tredway, L., & Stern, J. (2003, April). *"A job too big for one": Multiple principals and other approaches to school leadership.* Paper presented at the annual meeting of the American Educational Research Association, Chicago.

Hallinger, P., & Heck, R. H. (1996). Reassessing the principal's role in school effectiveness: A review of the empirical research. *Educational Administration Quarterly, 32*(1), 27–31.

Halverson, R. (2002). *Representing phronesis: Supporting instructional leadership practice in schools.* Unpublished doctoral dissertation, Northwestern University, Evanston, IL.

Hargreaves, A. (1991). *Restructuring restructuring: Postmodernity and the prospects for educational change.* Paper presented at the annual meeting of the American Educational Research Association, Chicago.

Hargreaves, A., & Fink, D. (2004, April). The seven principles of sustainable leadership. *Educational Leadership, 61*(7), 8–13.

Harris, A. (2002). Effective leadership in schools facing challenging contexts. *School Leadership and Management, 22*(1), 15–26.

Harris, A. (2005). Distributed leadership. In B. Davies (Ed.), *The essentials of school leadership* (pp. 173–190). London: Paul Chapman.

Harris, A., & Lambert, L. (2003). *Building leadership capacity for school improvement*. Milton Keynes, U.K.: Open University Press.

Heck, R., & Hallinger, P. (1999). Next generation methods for the study of leadership and school improvement. In J. Murphy & K. Louis (Eds.), *Handbook of Research on Educational Administration* (pp. 141–162). San Francisco: Jossey-Bass.

Heenan, D. A., & Bennis, W. (1999). *Co-leaders: The power of great partnerships*. New York: Wiley.

Heifetz, R. A. (1994). *Leadership without easy answers*. Cambridge, MA: Belknap Press.

Heller, M. F., & Firestone, W. A. (1995). Who's in charge here? Sources of leadership for change in eight schools. *Elementary School Journal*, 96(1), 65–86.

Hess, G. A. (2000). *Changes in students' achievement in Illinois and Chicago, 1990–2000*. Washington, DC: Brookings Institution.

Hollander, E. P. (1978). *Leadership dynamics: A practical guide to effective relationships*. New York: Free Press.

Hughes, M., & Busch, T. (1991). Theory and research as catalysts for change. In W. W. Walker, R. Farquhar, & M. Hughes (Eds.), *Advancing education: School leadership in action* (pp. 86–124). London: Falmer Press.

Johnson, G. S., & Venable, B. P. (1986). A study of teacher loyalty to the principal: Rule administration and hierarchical influence of the principal. *Educational Administration Quarterly*, 22(4), 4–28.

Johnson, S. M. (1990). *Teachers at work: Achieving success in our schools*. New York: Basic Books.

Katz, D., & Kahn, R. L. (1966). *The social psychology of organizations*. New York: Wiley.

Lawrence, P. R., & Lorsch, J. W. (1986). *Organization and environment: Managing differentiation and integration*. Boston: Harvard Business School Press.

Leithwood, K., Begley, P. T., & Cousins, J. B. (1992). *Developing expert leadership for future schools*. London: Falmer Press.

Liberman, A., Falk, B., & Alexander, L. (1994). *A culture in the making: Leadership in learner-centered schools*. New York:

National Center for Restructuring Education, Schools, and Teaching, Teachers College.

Little, J. W. (1982). Norms of collegiality and experimentation: Workplace conditions of school success. *American Educational Research Journal, 19*, 325–340.

Little, J. W. (1990). Conditions of professional development in secondary schools. In M. W. McLaughlin, J. E. Talbert, & N. Bascia (Eds.), *The contexts of teaching in secondary schools* (pp. 187–223). New York: Teachers College Press.

Little, J. W. (1993). Professional community in comprehensive high schools: The two worlds of academic and vocational teachers. In J. W. Little & M. W. McLaughlin (Eds.), *Teachers' work: Individuals, colleagues, and contexts* (pp. 137–163). New York: Teachers College Press.

Lortie, D. C. (1975). *Schoolteacher: A sociological study.* Chicago: University of Chicago Press.

Louis, K. S., Marks, H., & Kruse, S. (1996). Teachers' professional community in restructuring schools. *American Educational Research Journal, 33*(4), 757–798.

Malone, T., & Crowston, K. (1994). The interdisciplinary study of coordination. *ACM Computing Surveys, 26*, 87–119.

Malone, T. W., Crowston, K., Lee, J., Pentland, B., Dellarocas, C., Wyner, G., Quimby, J., Osborn, C. S., Bernstein, A., Herman, G., Klein, M., & O'Donnell, E. (1999). Tools for inventing organizations: Toward a handbook of organizational processes. *Management Science, 45*, 425–443.

March, J., & Simon, H. (1958). *Organizations.* New York: Wiley.

March, J. G., & Olsen, J. (1984). The new institutionalism: Organizational factors in political life. *American Political Science Review, 78*(3), 734–749.

Murphy, J. (1991). *Restructuring schools: Capturing and assessing the phenomena.* New York: Teachers College Press.

Norman, D. A. (1988). *The design of everyday things.* New York: Doubleday.

Perkins, D. N. (1986). *Knowledge as design.* Hillsdale, NJ: Erlbaum.

Portin, B., Schneider, P., DeArmond, M., & Gundlach, L. (2003). *Making sense of leading schools: A study of the school principalship.* Seattle: Center for Reinventing Public Education, University of Washington.

Rogoff, B., Turkanis, C. G., & Bartlett, L. (Eds.). (2001). *Learning together: Children and adults in a school community*. New York: Oxford University Press.

Rosenholtz, S. J. (1989). *Teachers' workplace: The social organization of schools*. New York: Longman.

Salomon, G., & Perkins, D. N. (1998). Individual and social aspects of learning. *Review of research in education, 23*, 1–24.

Schön, D. (1988). *Educating the reflective practitioner*. San Francisco: Jossey-Bass.

Shulman, L. S. (1986). Those who understand: Knowledge growth in teaching. *Educational Research, 15*(2), 4–14.

Shulman, L. S. (1987). Knowledge and teaching: Foundations of the new reform. *Harvard Educational Review, 57*(1), 1–22.

Siskin, L. S. (1994). *Realms of knowledge: Academic departments in secondary schools*. Washington, DC: Falmer Press.

Smylie, M. A., & Denny, J. W. (1990). Teacher leadership: Tensions and ambiguities in organizational perspectives. *Educational Administration Quarterly, 26*(3), 235–259.

Smylie, M. A., & Hart, A. W. (1999). School leadership for teacher learning and change: A human and social capital development perspective. In J. Murphy and K. S. Louis (Eds.), *Handbook of educational administration: A project of the American Educational Research Association* (pp. 421–442). San Francisco: Jossey-Bass.

Spillane, J. P. (2000). Cognition and policy implementation: District policymakers and the reform of mathematics education. *Cognition and Instruction, 18*(2), 141–179.

Spillane, J. (2005). Primary school leadership practice: How the subject matters. *School Leadership and Management, 24*(4), 383–397.

Spillane, J., Diamond, J., & Jita, L. (2000, April). *Leading classroom instruction: A preliminary exploration of the distribution of leadership practice*. Paper presented at the annual meeting of the American Educational Research Association, New Orleans.

Spillane, J. P., Diamond, J. B., & Jita, L. (2003). Leading instruction: The distribution of leadership for instruction. *Journal of Curriculum Studies, 35*(5), 533–543.

Spillane, J., Diamond, J., Sherer, J., & Coldren, A. (2004). Distributing leadership. In M. Coles & G. Southworth (Eds.), *Developing leadership: Creating the schools of tomorrow* (pp. 37–49). New York: Open University Press.

Spillane, J. P., Hallett, T., & Diamond, J. B. (2003). Forms of capital and the construction of leadership: Instructional leadership in urban elementary schools. *Sociology of Education, 76*(1), 1–17.

Spillane, J. P., Halverson, R., & Diamond, J. B. (2001). *Towards a theory of leadership practice: A distributed perspective.* (Institute for Policy Research Working Paper WP-99-3). Evanston, IL: Northwestern University.

Spillane, J., Halverson, R., & Diamond, J. (2004). Towards a theory of school leadership practice: Implications of a distributed perspective. *Journal of Curriculum Studies, 36*(1), 3–34.

Spillane, J., Sherer, J., & Coldren, A. (in press). Distributed leadership: Leadership practice and the situation. In W. Hoy & C. Miskil (Eds.), *Educational Leadership and Reform* (pp. 149–167). New York: IAP Publishing.

Stodolsky, S. (1988). *The subject matters.* Chicago: University of Chicago Press.

Stodolsky, S. (1989). Is teaching really by the books? *Yearbook of the National Society for the Study of Education, 88,* 159–184.

Stodolsky, S., & Grossman, P. L. (1995). The impact of subject matter on curricular activity: An analysis of five academic subjects. *American Educational Research Journal, 32*(2), 227–249.

Thompson, J. D. (1967). *Organizations in action: Social science bases of administrative theory.* New York: McGraw-Hill.

Treslan, D. L., & Ryan, J. J. (1986). Perceptions of principals' influence bases. *Canadian Administrator, 26*(2), 1–7.

Tucker, R. C. (1981). *Politics as leadership.* Columbia: University of Missouri Press.

Weick, K. E., & Roberts, K. H. (1993). Collective mind in organizations: Heedful interrelating on flight decks. *Administrative Science Quarterly, 38*(3), 357–381.

Wertsch, J. V. (1998). *Mind as action.* New York: Oxford University Press.

Wood, P. (2004). Democratic leadership: Drawing distinctions with distributed leadership. *International Journal of Leadership in Education, 7*(1), 3–26.

Yukl, G. (1999). An evaluation of conceptual weaknesses in transformational and charismatic leadership theories. *Leadership Quarterly, 10*(2), 285–305.

Index

TITLES IN THE JOSSEY-BASS LEADERSHIP LIBRARY IN EDUCATION SERIES

Andy Hargreaves, Dean Fink, **Sustainable Leadership**

In *Sustainable Leadership*, Andy Hargreaves and Dean Fink address one of the most important and often neglected aspects of leadership: sustainability. The authors set out a compelling and original framework of seven principles for sustainable leadership characterized by Depth of learning and real achievement rather than superficially tested performance; Length of impact over the long haul, beyond individual leaders, through effectively managed succession; Breadth of influence, where leadership becomes a distributed responsibility; Justice in ensuring that leadership actions do no harm to and actively benefit students in other schools; Diversity that replaces standardization and alignment with diversity and cohesion; Resourcefulness that conserves and renews leaders' energy and doesn't burn them out; and Conservation that builds on the best of the past to create an even better future.

ISBN 0-7879-6838-2   Paperback   352 Pages   2005

Ann Lieberman, Lynne Miller, **Teacher Leadership**

Teacher Leadership is written for teachers who assume responsibility for educational success beyond their own classrooms by providing peer support, modeling good practice, or coordinating curriculum and instruction. It offers cases studies of innovative programs and stories of individual teachers who lead in a variety of contexts. It shows how to develop learning communities that include rather than exclude, create knowledge rather than merely applying it, and provide challenge and support to new and experienced teachers.

ISBN 0-7879-6245-7   Paperback   112 Pages   2004

James Ryan, **Inclusive Leadership**

This is an innovative and groundbreaking book about the powerful new idea of inclusive leadership. The culture of schools and the diversity of those who lead them have not kept pace with the growing diversity in the student population. James Ryan's work focuses on leadership as an intentionally inclusive practice that values all cultures and types of students and educators in a school. He looks upon leadership as a collective influence process to promote inclusion. In four chapters, Ryan provides an overview of the topic, a summary of research, examples of good practice, and guidelines for the future.

ISBN 0-7879-6508-1   Paperback   208 Pages   2005

Robert J. Starratt, **Ethical Leadership**

In *Ethical Leadership*, Robert Starratt—one of the leading thinkers on the topic of ethics and education—shows educational leaders how to move beyond mere technical efficiency in the delivery and performance of learning. He explains that leadership requires a moral commitment to high quality learning, based on three essential virtues: proactive responsibility, personal and professional authenticity, and an affirming, critical, and enabling presence.

ISBN 0-7879-6564-2   Paperback   176 Pages   2004

Michael Fullan, **Turnaround Leadership**

ISBN 0-7879-6985-0   Paperback   128 Pages (approx.)   Fall 2006

Geoffrey Southworth, **Learner-Centered Leadership**

ISBN 0-7879-7553-2   Paperback   128 Pages (approx.)   Fall 2006

CPSIA information can be obtained
at www.ICGtesting.com
Printed in the USA
FSHW010622090421
80224FS